Missing

A Memoir

LINDSAY HARRISON

Scribner

New York London Toronto Sydney

Scribner
A Division of Simon & Schuster, Inc.
1230 Avenue of the Americas
New York, NY 10020

Some names and identifying characteristics have been changed.

First Scribner hardcover edition August 2011

SCRIBNER and design are registered trademarks of The Gale Group, Inc. used under license by Simon & Schuster, Inc., the publisher of this work.

For information about special discounts for bulk purchases, please contact Simon & Schuster Special Sales at 1-866-506-1949 or business@simonandschuster.com.

The Simon & Schuster Speakers Bureau can bring authors to your live event. For more information or to book an event contact the Simon & Schuster Speakers Bureau at 1-866-248-3049 or visit our website at www.simonspeakers.com.

Manufactured in the United States of America

1   3   5   7   9   10   8   6   4   2

Library of Congress Cataloging-in-Publication Data

Harrison, Lindsay, 1985–
Missing : a memoir / Lindsay Harrison.—1st Scribner hardcover ed.
        p. cm.
1. Harrison, Lindsay, 1985—Family. I. Title.
CT275.H38645 A3 2011
974.4'043092—dc22
[B]
2011005572

ISBN 978-1-4516-1193-9
ISBN 978-1-4516-1198-4 (ebook)

For my family,
of course

Missing

Chapter One

AFTER THE ARGUMENT with my mom, everything started spinning. Tilt-a-Whirl vertigo. Hoping a prescription for glasses would make the world appear the way it should again, I made an appointment with the optometrist for the morning of Friday, March 17, 2006.

The receptionist led me to a small examining room down the hall. The doctor had me read the eye chart, then asked me to identify a series of letters through various lenses. He dilated my pupils and checked the backs of my eyes. My vision, he declared, was twenty-twenty.

"Then why does everything keep spinning?" I asked.

"It's probably neurological. You'd have to get more tests to know."

I walked back to campus wondering what kind of disorders he had in mind. Turning off Waterman Street, I passed through the brick archway leading into Brown's campus. Students were streaming to and from class, pouring out of buildings, playing Frisbee on the muddy quad. My cell phone started ringing and I hoped it was my mom calling me back. Normally I talked to her a few times a day. I thought of her as my best friend as much as my mother.

But everything had changed three months earlier: New Year's Eve, my twentieth birthday. I'd chosen to spend the night with college friends instead of with my mom, and it had cost me. She'd thrown me out of her apartment the next day, and our argument had ended in my father's driveway, where she stopped the car only long enough to toss my clothes onto his lawn and tell me that this was what I'd wanted. Since then she hadn't answered my phone calls and I'd seen her only twice.

My sophomore spring had been marked by mysterious bouts of vertigo. I kept hoping my mom would stop being so stubborn and just call me back. I reached for my phone as I cut across the quad toward my art history class, which started in five minutes.

My brother's name appeared on the caller ID.

"Have you talked to Mom today?" Brad asked.

"No, why?"

"Her boss called and said she didn't show up for work."

"Maybe she went to New Hampshire. I have class now."

"You have to get home."

"Seriously?"

But he didn't have to tell me twice. Immediately I knew something was wrong. My two older brothers and I always knew where our mom was. We talked to her morning, noon, and night; even at work, she never silenced or shut off her cell phone. While we were growing up, she'd attended every sporting event and school function, juggling a full-time teaching job as a divorcée with primary custody of my brothers and me. Until our overblown argument on New Year's Eve, she'd been completely dependable and I could always reach her.

She was never late. If she needed to call in sick, she did so by six a.m. This was the first time in fifteen years that her boss had to dig up her emergency contact info, which listed Barbara Ann—our mother's closest friend from the Massachusetts suburb where we'd grown up—as the person to call if something was wrong. Barbara Ann had called Brad, who immediately called our older brother, Chris, and me.

"Go now, Lindsay."

My family refers to me by my full name only when there's a problem.

"I have to take an exam at one. I'm leaving as soon as I finish," he said.

A junior at Cornell, Brad was sequestered in upstate New York and his drive home was at least eight hours. I could make it from Rhode Island to Mom's apartment in Massachusetts in two and a half hours by train. Considering I didn't have a three-hour economics midterm to suffer through first, I knew I better get going.

Students strode by me as I stumbled to a nearby bench. I could feel another round of vertigo coming on, the ground swooping up to meet the sky. The four barrels lining the path started to spin: Trash, Paper, Bottles, and Mixed Containers. I shut my eyes to still the chaos. I gripped the edge of the bench and waited for my best friend Cassidy to meet me before class, like always.

"What's wrong?" she said. "You look sick."

The bells rang out, signaling twelve o'clock classes.

"I can't go to class."

"Why not?"

The last of the stragglers disappeared into buildings around the main green as I told her about my mom not showing up for work. We hurried off toward our dorm. Cassidy and I had met a year and a half earlier in an art class. She'd arrived from Vermont with a unicycle and an old guitar, which was enough to impress me. Sophomore year we were sharing a dorm room and trading thrift store T-shirts and beaded necklaces.

I threw my toothbrush and a change of clothes into my backpack. Cassidy looked up the train schedule online.

"The next one leaves at one thirty. C'mon, you should eat first," she said.

We went to the dining hall and I got my usual meal of salad and Diet Coke. The students around us were maddeningly carefree with their soft-serve cones and their campus newspapers. Instead of waiting around for the train, I felt like I should be hitting the road immediately, borrowing a friend's car or hitchhiking. I stabbed a fork at my lettuce as the dread in my stomach turned to nausea. Cassidy kept saying it would all be fine. I pushed my plate away and looked up at the oversize clock on the wall. I wanted to believe her, but the minutes were moving toward one o'clock impossibly slowly.

Cassidy reached for my hand as we walked downtown to the train station, her fingers glinting with the silver rings she always wore. My backpack thumped against my spine. I wanted to be overreacting, wanted this to be a false alarm, but something in Brad's voice had faltered from his usual tough-guy stoicism.

I hugged Cassidy and bought a ticket for the northbound train.

"I'm sure it's just a misunderstanding," she called across the terminal.

The train was packed with people leaving Providence for the weekend. I took the window seat beside a blue-suited businessman and began scrolling through the contacts saved in my cell phone. Starting with the A's and working my way through the alphabet, I called friends and relatives—many of whom I hadn't spoken to in months, if not years—to ask if they'd heard from my mother lately or happened to know where she was. I tried to sound casual. I phoned old friends we'd sailed with every summer in Rhode Island, soccer moms from our hometown of North Andover, and the neighbor across the hall in Mom's apartment building in Newburyport. I called information to track down more numbers. Her friends were quick to assure me that she probably just needed a long weekend away. I thanked them and moved down the list, feeling dizzy and trapped on the slow-moving train. My phone started to beep. I called my brother Chris and told him to pick me up at the Newburyport station. He'd left his office job in Boston and rushed to Mom's apartment as soon as Brad had called a few hours earlier.

I sat pinned against the window, restless at every stop. My phone battery died halfway down the list of people who might have said, "Your mother is right here." After an hour the train reached South Station in Boston: the end of the line. I got off and transferred to the Newburyport line, anxious to keep going. Another hour ticked by as the second train slid up along the coast, finally pulling into Newburyport. I was the first one off the platform.

Chris honked from the parking lot and I ran over and got into his Ford Explorer. He'd been pacing our mom's apartment for the past few hours, trying to figure out where she'd gone. The driveway was empty; her car wasn't there. Chris said he'd even called the police, but they told him a person wasn't officially considered missing until seventy-two hours had passed, unless we had reason to suspect a crime had been committed. Even after Chris explained that skipping work was extremely unusual of our mother, the police officer said there was nothing he could do until Monday. We should try to relax; she probably just went away for the weekend.

But even as Chris told me that he'd called the police, I resisted the idea of involving them. As scary as it was to not know our mother's whereabouts, I had no doubt that my brothers and I would find her. We knew her patterns and all the likely places she might have gone. Beyond her unswerving reliability, Mom had raised us in an air of intense privacy; as kids we weren't supposed to tell anyone that our parents were divorced. Calling old friends to ask if they'd recently seen her made me feel like I was breaking her rules, but already I could sense that something more important had snapped.

As soon as I got in the car, Chris handed me our mom's red suede purse, saying he'd found it in her apartment. Mom had given me this bag for Christmas two years earlier, and I'd returned it to her when I grew tired of it.

"Start looking through there," Chris said.

"She always takes her purse."

"I know."

"What am I looking for?"

"Just look, Lindsay!"

At twenty-four, Chris was four years older than me, old enough to boss me around. He resembled our mom more than Brad and I did, with his narrow nose and chestnut hair, his kindness and quick temper. I started digging. Mom's Wet n Wild lipstick was down to a dark red stub. I sifted through her drugstore reading glasses, a scattering of receipts and blank sticky notes, a handful of spare change, a hairbrush tangled with strands of dyed brown hair, a bottle of beige foundation, and her black wallet, bulging with credit cards, small bills, and creased photographs of my brothers and me. I couldn't imagine where she would be going without all her essentials. I threw the bag on the floor and told Chris to drive faster.

A few minutes later we pulled into the driveway of the white clapboard house on High Street. Mom had been living in an apartment on the third floor for the past year and a half. I'd been preparing to leave for my first semester of college when she announced that she was done with North Andover.

"The boys are gone and you're leaving too. Why would I want this big old house anymore?" she'd said at the time.

So Mom sold the house we'd grown up in amid talk of starting over. She rented an apartment in Newburyport, a picturesque coastal town forty minutes from North Andover, where she planned to make new friends, find romance, lose weight, and do the things that amount to a second chance. We didn't know anyone in Newburyport and weren't sure why she was moving to a town that would double her commute to Woburn, where she worked as a special education teacher. My brothers and I didn't question her motives, though. With the ocean just down the road, her wood-beamed apartment seemed like a fitting place to start over. If Mom had any fears about a new beginning, she kept them to herself.

I took the stairs two at a time, up three flights, and reached for the spare key above the door frame. I threw open the door wanting to believe that Mom would be waiting on the other side, ready to put this whole misunderstanding behind us. The apartment was cluttered, same as always—books stacked beside the couch, an empty coffee mug on the table, and Mom's brown corduroy blazer draped over the back of a chair. It looked like she had just run out to the store. Needed eggs, maybe milk. Like she'd be right back.

But her key chain was hanging on the hook in the kitchen, crammed with at least ten keys, including the one for the Subaru Outback she'd bought a few months earlier. I never understood why she toted so many keys—I couldn't imagine what they all opened—but along with her purse, Mom took this hefty ring wherever she went.

"Chris, did you see this?" I said.

"She must've taken her spare car key."

"Then she won't be gone long."

After plugging my cell phone in to charge it, I emptied the purse and made a paper trail of receipts and sticky notes, trying to retrace our mom's footsteps. A crumpled receipt from an Irving gas station near her office in Woburn, her Visa card swiped at seven fifteen a.m. on Thursday, March 16. This implied that she'd gotten to work the day before about a half hour earlier than the other teachers, who came in at eight. My mother was always punctual and often early, but never late. Her boss was alarmed enough to dig up her emergency contact info when she didn't show up by midmorning.

A receipt for groceries purchased at Market Basket four days earlier: milk, cheese, hummus, and French bread. Photos developed at CVS, a whole roll shot on the sand dunes of Plum Island, a barrier island between Newburyport Harbor and the Atlantic Ocean: sunsets, driftwood, and fishermen casting offshore. It all fit into her routine. I was about to give up and hurl the empty purse across the room when I noticed one more receipt, folded and tucked in an inner pocket.

"Chris—"

"What'd you find?"

"A receipt for a Budget rental truck."

The yellow copy, dated Wednesday, March 15, made more sense to my brother than it did to me. Apparently the moving truck was all part of the plan. Mom had recently bought a house in the White Mountains of New Hampshire, fifteen minutes south of the ski condo where we'd vacationed for years. After almost two decades of working as a special education teaching associate, our mother was looking forward to an early retirement within a few years. The apartment in Newburyport was never supposed to be permanent; she was just taking some time to figure out where she wanted to settle down. Brad had planned to drive home on his upcoming spring break to help Mom transport a storage unit full of furniture to her new house. The truck was scheduled to be picked up the following week.

I had always envisioned my mother by the sea—she had dreamed of running a bed-and-breakfast on a Rhode Island bluff we sailed past every summer—but she took a turn for the mountains instead. Normally she included me in every decision, right down to making the grocery list. But things had changed since our New Year's Eve fight. We'd barely spoken since, and I knew next to nothing about the house she'd bought. Still, I hoped that's where she had gone.

Chris called Budget rental and learned that Mom hadn't picked up the truck early. My next thought was that she'd gotten in her car and driven north, wanting to map out the furniture arrangement in her new house or shop at the nearby outlet stores. Maybe her cell phone had run out of battery power en route. She would plug it in and call one of my brothers or me when she got there, but the worry was in the waiting. She phoned at least one of us every morning by the time she got to work. She was my morning alarm, and instead of saying prayers at night, I talked to her.

Chris had already called 411 and requested the phone number of our mother's future neighbors in New Hampshire. Once connected, he introduced himself and asked if they'd seen any cars in the dirt driveway beyond their barn. Any lights on in the windows? They said the property looked deserted but promised to keep a lookout. The Budget receipt implied that Mom was following a plan, one she'd eagerly shared with my brothers and the details of which she'd stubbornly kept from me in the wake of our argument. Even if I didn't know where the house was located or what it looked like, a house in the mountains made enough sense. For the past few years Mom had been saying she needed to simplify. Glancing up at the wooden plaque above her bedroom door that said just that, I held on to the yellow scrap of paper as if it were proof that everything was still moving toward a straightforward explanation.

There was also the possibility that she hadn't gone north yet. Maybe she was just playing hooky and would come walking into the apartment any second. She would apologize for making us worry and relay an amusing story about her day off. Since this seemed just as likely, we decided to wait it out. Instead of chasing after her, it made more sense to remain at home base and wait for her to come back.

Brad got on the road at four, right after finishing his midterm. He had transferred from Boston College—Mom's alma mater—to Cornell for his junior year. He called Chris and me at least ten times during his ride. We leaped for our cell phones, thinking Brad was about to say that he'd gotten hold of Mom, while he was hoping to hear that she'd just walked into the apartment. As the hours wore on, the calls became our way to keep Brad awake on his drive. After feeling exhausted for weeks, he had finally gone to the doctor a few days before. Tests revealed that he had mono, which explained his fatigue, fever, and sore throat. We were worried that he would fall asleep at the wheel and end up in a field full of cows.

On his sixth or seventh call, Brad told us to go to every gas station that Mom might stop at on her way out of town. He was hoping they'd have security cameras, hoping for a video clip showing a white station wagon pulling into the frame and a fifty-three-year-old woman pumping gas. How it would tell us what direction Mom took or where she was heading, we didn't know. She'd bought a half tank the day before at the Irving station near her office, but we figured she'd top off if she were planning a getaway.

We left a note on the kitchen table before leaving:

Mom,
We came home to see you. Call us.
Love,
    C, B, and L

Mobil, Shell, Texaco, Getty—we checked all the Newburyport stations without any luck. The pumps were old and the signs displaying the prices had not yet gone digital. The thought of security cameras in such a quaint suburb was absurd. We got on I-95 north and looked for gas station symbols on the blue service signs that lined the road every few miles. Six p.m. and the sun had set without our noticing. The interstate pulsed with yellow headlights. We followed an exit toward a Getty station and entered the adjacent convenience store, where the clerk on duty was a few years younger than me. He flipped through the day's receipts to see if he could find one that matched our mother's credit card number, but we grew impatient watching him dig through the fat stack of paper slips.

"She drives a white Subaru Outback. Midfifties, five-four, chin-length brown hair, probably wearing jeans, looks like a mom. Anyone like that come through?" Chris asked.

"Lots of people come and go," he said.

"Do you videotape the pumps?"

"The tape's locked in the office, but the manager comes in at eleven."

"Think he'll be able to show us the tape?"

"Don't see why not."

"Okay, we'll come back then."

"Actually I might've seen someone who fit that description this afternoon."

Music to our ears. But even if our mother had passed through, it told us nothing about where she'd gone next. Still, it was something.

Chris and I got back in the car. We knew it was time to call our father. In the seventeen years since their divorce, our parents had never learned how to get along. Mom had done her best over the years to convince my brothers and me that her ex-husband was not a good man, and even less of a father.

"We have to tell him," Chris said.

"Fine. You call."

He was probably in the middle of dinner, but like our mother, Dad always answered the phone.

"Dad, it's Chris. Something's wrong."

"What?"

"It's our mom."

"What about her?"

"We can't find her."

"Can't *find* her?"

"She didn't show up for work. We've been looking for her all day."

"She's probably up at your ski condo."

"She's not there," Chris said. "Brad's driving home from Cornell and Lindsay's with me."

"Call me tomorrow. I'm sure you'll hear from her by then," Dad said before hanging up.

Chris slammed his fist on the dashboard. "He thinks we're overreacting."

"What did you expect?"

Chris swallowed whatever he was about to say and looked out the window. I knew Dad wouldn't share our immediate alarm. Our mother was hardly his favorite person. It baffled me that my parents had been married for almost two decades. Mom acted out of emotion, Dad out of logic. He was a Princeton man, an engineer, and then president and CEO of a high-tech company until selling it at the age of fifty. He had also married another woman whose name was the same as my mother's: Michele. An unfortunate coincidence as well as a constant reminder to my mom that she had been replaced.

Dad and his new wife lived in a beachfront mansion along with their beautiful towheaded child, Maggie. At fourteen years old, I suddenly had a new sibling. In my mother's eyes, this was against the rules. A man was supposed to have only one wife, one set of kids. Even as my mom was so keen on starting over, it seemed she had never forgiven her ex-husband for seizing his own second chance.

Dad's version of starting over included undertaking the restoration of an enormous old house as well as an early retirement so that he could be a stay-at-home parent. When he wasn't occupied with Maggie, Dad was building cabinets, gutting bedrooms, landscaping, and otherwise trying to restore his property to a Gatsbyesque splendor it hadn't seen in decades. He was a Renaissance man, still as fit and handsome as he was when my mother met him in college. His eyes were the same deep blue as the waves that broke on West Beach, right outside his bedroom window. By all outward appearances, his second chance had panned out quite nicely.

Chris and I drove around Newburyport for a while, checking parking lots for a white Subaru while speculating about where our mom could have gone. We went back and checked her apartment for any clues we might have overlooked. We called her cell phone several more times, but it continued to go straight to voice mail.

Even though we still had at least an hour before we could view the gas station video, we got back in the car. Being on the move was easier on our nerves than sitting in the apartment; we were hoping to spot Mom's station wagon or even pass her on the road.

But it was hard to tell what kinds of cars we were passing. March in New England meant the sun went down by six p.m. and the only light thereafter came from headlights, an indifferent moon, and a smattering of stars. Chris pulled into a liquor store parking lot off the highway. The adrenaline-pumped afternoon had collapsed into utter fatigue. Worrying was tiring. We reclined our seats, hoping to rest until eleven o'clock or until Brad called again, whichever came first. He'd been driving straight for the past six hours and had about two more to go. I shut my eyes, but I was no closer to sleep when a policeman rapped on the driver's-side window and beamed a flashlight in our eyes. Chris rolled down the window and we both sat up a little straighter.

We knew the officer would be of no use until several more hours passed, so there seemed little point in explaining our predicament. Easier to just let him assume we were causing trouble outside a liquor store on a Friday night. We rolled up the windows and got back on the road, and for a few minutes I hated the cop, even though he'd done nothing wrong. It never crossed my mind to turn my frustrations on my mother, who had put us in this situation in the first place.

Ten thirty. We cruised through Newburyport, past the boardwalk and the waterfront restaurants, looping through the brick-faced center of town for the fifth or sixth time. Everything was closed. Coming up on eleven, we drove back to the Getty station.

The same kid was sitting behind the counter, no manager in sight. Apparently the manager was taking the night off and had forgotten to press the Record button on the camera that morning. The attendant told us this without looking up from his magazine. We got back to Mom's apartment just before midnight.

We did our best to not wake the neighbors, but the wooden stairs groaned and our footsteps echoed up through the halls. We opened the front door, willing Mom to be dozing in her easy chair, feet up on the ottoman, wineglass on the end table. But the lights were just the lamps we had turned on before leaving.

We called Brad to tell him about the dead ends we'd run into at the gas stations. He was still a half hour away, and I pictured him cruising in the fast lane, palming the steering wheel while going over the possibilities for the hundredth time: her new house, a weekend getaway, a dead cell phone battery, an explanation that would make perfect sense when she returned. Even as he told himself to stay calm, I knew he was as scared as he'd ever been, a fire-alarm fear difficult to explain to anyone but Chris and me—because we felt it too. It was completely out of character for our mom to take off without telling us. Her mood swings could be brutal, but her temper always cooled quickly, and she was nothing if not consistent in phone calls, care packages, and visits. She was the glue that held us all together.

I crawled into my mother's bed, searching for her body's indentation. Chris lay on the couch, a trail of receipts stretching across the floor in front of him. We called out to each other in the dark.

"She probably just went away for the weekend," I said.

"It'll make sense in the morning," he replied.

Neither of us sounded convinced. I pulled the blankets up under my chin. Minutes or hours passed with the faint whoosh of cars on High Street and the dim beam of headlights across the ceiling, like signals from an erratic lighthouse. I finally fell asleep, tangled in the roses of my mother's sheets.

Chapter Two

I WOKE AT SEVEN in the morning with the brief hope that the past twenty-four hours had all been a bad dream. Then I realized I was in my mom's bed and not my own. I got up and pulled on yesterday's jeans. Chris was asleep on the couch and Brad was splayed out on the floral-print armchair. Fourteen months older than me, Brad and I had the same almost black hair, thick eyebrows, and slightly sloped noses—our father's features. At six-two, both of my brothers were too tall to sleep comfortably on couches and chairs, but being the only girl, I got the bed without question.

I hesitated for a moment before waking them. Even asleep, Brad looked exhausted. His hair was greasy, his face sallow and unshaved, his T-shirt and Carhartts rumpled and dirty. Mono was taking its toll on his rower's body; he was looking a little skinny. I'd been asleep when he'd arrived, sometime after midnight.

"Guys, get up," I said.

"Is Mom here?" Chris asked.

"No."

We moved quickly, tying our shoes and grabbing the car keys without bothering to brush our teeth or change into clean clothes. We didn't have a plan, but sleeping in or sitting around would've been inexcusable. Chris drove while Brad and I scanned the sidewalks where our mom liked to walk along the waterfront. We checked all the likely places in town, scanning parking spots for her Subaru. The bank, post office, and library—where she often went to use the Internet—were not yet open, and we would come back to check these places in a few hours. We stopped at Dunkin' Donuts and drove back to Mom's apartment. Already the idea that we would spot her taking a stroll through town seemed too simple. If she were doing that, she would be on the phone chatting with one of us.

We called our mom's old friend Barbara Ann and asked her when they'd last spoken. An hour later, Barbara Ann was knocking on the front door, her husband and three adult children in tow. As the first person notified when our mother failed to show up for work, she was as concerned as we were.

"How can we help?" she asked.

We had grown up with her kids at sporting events, pool parties, and sleepovers. Barbara Ann and her husband had always gone out of their way to make life a little easier for their divorced friend with three kids. But our latest request was a little different from giving us a ride home from soccer practice.

We split into teams. It was almost like playing an elaborate game of hide-and-seek. Chris's team would check our grandmother's nursing home in Natick, where Mom visited almost every day after work. Brad's team would drive to Mom's new house and our ski condo in New Hampshire. Barbara Ann's husband and son were going to North Andover to scout our old neighborhood. Barbara Ann and I would search Plum Island. We were operating on the belief that hide-and-seek players usually end up in the same tried-and-true spots.

Barbara Ann drove through town and turned toward the island. The last time I'd been on this road, I was with my mom, cruising to the beach in our old Saab convertible. We had gone almost every afternoon the previous summer. The island was accessible only by one road, a single lane that wound past a few small planes at the sleepy airport, straightened out through the salt marshes, and led up and over a metal drawbridge.

My mom often drove to Plum Island after going to work and the nursing home. She'd sit and read in her beach chair or walk the shore with her camera, looking for serenity after the stress of working with handicapped young adults at her teaching collaborative. Placed at various companies over the years and most recently at a technology company called Skyworks, the teachers aimed to integrate students into the workforce. For almost a decade my mom had been working one-on-one with a handicapped student named Cynthia, who in addition to her learning disabilities was also losing her eyesight. She could perform repetitive office tasks only under the guidance of my mother.

In her early twenties, Cynthia was around the same age as my brothers and me. In the mornings they would open the office mail together: my mother with a letter opener, slicing and sliding the envelope to Cynthia, who would unfold and stack the contents, recycle the envelope, and reach for the next. Hands slicing, sliding, opening, and unfolding, "like watching a symphony orchestra," one of her colleagues would later tell me. Cynthia was almost completely blind by this point, and my mother had become her eyes as well as her second set of hands. She could anticipate when Cynthia had a seizure coming on and would take her outside to walk around the parking lot, which more often than not would calm her down.

Worrying about Cynthia's deteriorating condition and the monotony of her training had been wearing on my mom for years. But once she reached the island and stuck her toes in the sand, she was free. My mom had grown up sailing and passed on a love of the Atlantic to my brothers and me; every summer we'd cast off the bowlines on our old wooden sailboat, *Pippins,* motoring out of a marina in Rhode Island and tacking across Narragansett Bay. But as my brothers and I reached adolescence, sports and summer jobs gained precedence, and we took *Pippins* out of the water indefinitely.

Walking the shore of Plum Island, Mom always called me, and if I didn't answer, she'd hold her cell phone to the waves and leave a message without saying a word. One hundred miles south in Providence, I'd press the phone to my ear, hear the dull roar of the waves, and know just where she was.

Barbara Ann and I drove toward the barren island in silence. It was the first time I had been there in the off-season. The waterways carved through the salt marsh were dotted with ice floes, and the swath of black water beneath the bridge looked too narrow for a boat to pass. Halfway into March, the island was still gripped by winter.

We rumbled over the metal bridge and past the WELCOME TO

PLUM ISLAND sign. Up on the left was a boarded-up shack, wedged between the road and the mudflats. The place had been painted, patched, and finally, abandoned. Across the side hung a banner: NO EVACUATION POSSIBLE.

Neither of us said anything as we passed. I kept glancing in the rearview mirror, unnerved by what seemed to be a bad omen. The seat belt tightened against my ribs as Barbara Ann made a hard right.

We pulled up to the entrance hut for the Parker River Wildlife Refuge, but there wouldn't be a ranger on duty for at least another month, so we drove around the barrier without paying our dues. The bird sanctuary was all twists and turns, bordered on the Atlantic side by scrub-covered sand dunes, and by dense trees and vegetation on the bay side. The southern half of the island was a protected habitat for hundreds of species, but most of the birds had not yet returned from their winter migrations, and it felt like driving through a dried-up swamp.

Mom always chose the quiet sanctuary over the touristy upper half of Plum Island. Whenever we went to the beach, she'd make us walk for what felt like miles before we could unfold our hot aluminum chairs and spread our towels, far from the other bathers.

Trees crowded the road, scrappy and bent by the coastal winds. I scanned the right-hand side of the road while Barbara Ann surveyed the left. There wasn't a bird-watcher in sight.

A smaller dirt road cut through the brush on our right. Barbara Ann stopped the car and I got out to unhook the rusty metal chain blocking the way. We wanted to go where we weren't supposed to, if only to feel like we'd thoroughly searched the place. The chances of Mom wandering the footpaths of the refuge seemed unlikely, given that it was cold and damp and the birds were still south. But searching meant breaking the rules, and if solitude was what she was looking for, this was a good place to find it.

We drove onto a bumpy dirt road that extended onto a peninsula above the marshland. Newburyport Harbor stretched out in the distance beyond the shack that had warned of no evacuation. This was the New England I knew, the landscape my mother loved. A desolate beauty: jagged ice floes in the water, a raw wind tangling the hardy beach grass, snow plowed in heaps along a dirt road, and not a person in sight. I loved it too.

"Shit!" Barbara Ann yelled.

The road crested over a dune and she slammed on the brakes at the lip of a ridge. Obscured by sand and snow, the end of the road had come without warning, and we were about to pitch forward into the icy water. I braced myself against the dashboard while Barbara Ann put the Ford in reverse and backed us away from the edge. We drove back to the mainland, barely mentioning the near catastrophe.

Our teams regrouped at Mom's apartment that afternoon. Brad had driven four hours to leave a note in the empty house in New Hampshire, unable to find traces of anyone having been there:

> Dear Mom,
> We really want to talk to you. If you're up
> here, please call us.
> Love,
> C, B, and L

North Andover had revealed nothing, and the nursing home, even less. Our eighty-seven-year-old grandmother hadn't yet realized that her daughter had missed three of her daily visits, although the nurses had taken note. Mom was among their most regular visitors, and the staff had grown friendly with her. They promised to call if she came by.

Barbara Ann and her family went home, saying they'd return in the morning. My brothers and I paced the apartment, trying to figure out what to do next. We still wanted to believe what everyone kept saying: that our mother had simply gone away for the weekend and had forgotten to check in. But it was hard to ignore the fact that we had just spent the entire day visiting all the likely places she would have gone.

Earlier that afternoon, Dad had called to apologize for not taking Chris and me seriously when we'd phoned him the night before. Although he was not on speaking terms with our mother, he knew how close we were to her and that if we didn't know where she was, no one would. He offered to search with us, but just as I still didn't think that we needed help from the police, I didn't want Dad to get involved.

That night I slept in my mom's bed again. I kept the bedroom door open so I could hear my brothers. Every time we heard footsteps, one of us ran to open the door and peer over the railing. But it was just the neighbors, their keys jangling as they entered their own apartments on the lower floors.

I woke up groggy on Sunday, remembered what was happening, and got up to wake my brothers. I checked my voice mail and called my mom while peeing. Searching required multitasking: things like bathroom breaks had to be justified. The longer our mother was gone, the farther from us she could be getting. Chasing after her had to be constant, if only to preserve the illusion that we were catching up.

Mom's cell phone went straight to an automated recording: "I'm sorry, but the person you are trying to reach is unavailable." We learned from Verizon that her phone had been off since Thursday night at seven thirty, just after Chris had called her. He racked his brain to remember any strange particulars of the conversation, but there wasn't much to report: Mom sounded tired and said she'd talk to him later.

If only she would turn her phone back on, Verizon could track the location of the nearest cell signal tower. She didn't even have to answer. Just let it ring. Verizon would track her and we'd race to where the treasure map was marked with an X. But I didn't want to find her that way. I wanted her to pick up. I wanted to tell her to come home. Wanted to hear her say, "I'm on my way."

When we weren't calling her phone, we were tracing credit cards. She hadn't taken her purse, which contained her wallet. Emptying her credit cards onto the kitchen table, we discovered that the only one missing was her Visa. Brad called customer service and finessed his way around the company's confidentiality policy. He could sweet-talk anyone: growing up, Brad had always acted as deal maker for Mom's big purchases—from new cars to our ski condo to the house she'd just bought in New Hampshire—as if he were her financial adviser rather than her teenage son.

If Mom had bought a plane ticket or charged a meal, we would have a clue to work with. But when Brad got off the phone a few minutes later, all he'd learned was that she hadn't used her credit card since buying gas at the Irving station on Thursday morning before work. The receipt lay on the floor. Our mom hardly ever paid in cash, but she hadn't charged anything in four days. It didn't make sense.

Maybe she had a secret stash of money, a billfold beneath the mattress or in a coffee can in the top cupboard. Maybe she'd been squirreling away funds for a getaway for a long time. It seemed just as unlikely as her disappearance.

My brothers and I kept reminding each other how hard it would be to completely fall off the radar in the age of cell phones, video cameras, and credit cards. If disappearing was what our mother wanted to do, although we couldn't fathom her reasons, we figured she would have to leave a footprint before long. We created an online account for her Visa card, hoping to catch her as soon as she made a purchase. We took turns sitting at the computer, hitting the Refresh button throughout the day, but nothing showed up.

There was something else, we suddenly realized, that would leave a trail whether Mom wanted to or not: her E-Z Pass transponder. There were three tolls on the way to New Hampshire, and we still believed that's where she'd gone. E-Z Pass kept a record of all its customers' transactions, complete with time and location of any toll deductions.

Despite Brad's tactics on the phone, which ranged from distraught son to angry customer, the E-Z Pass representative refused to disclose our mother's information. Brad begged. He asked to speak to the manager, who finally admitted that a recent charge was showing up on her account. Brad gave Chris and me a thumbs-up, but then his face clouded over again. The manager would not say when or where the transaction had taken place. Being given this fragment of information was maddening. It told us that Mom had taken a toll road, though we didn't know in which direction she was heading. There were tolls en route to New Hampshire, but practically every major highway had a toll at some point. We didn't know if she had left three days ago or only an hour before; she could have been sixty or six hundred miles from us.

When we were little, my brothers and I would puff our cheeks full of air whenever Mom drove through a tunnel, over a bridge, or past a graveyard. Whoever could hold his breath the longest was the winner. Nobody wanted to lose on the graveyard stretch, because giving up meant having to breathe death-infected air. Sitting in Mom's apartment more than a decade later, we didn't dare voice the question causing our lungs to burn as if we were playing that old car game again:

What if she doesn't come home tonight?

The day crawled toward night. I called Cassidy to tell her I didn't know when I'd be coming back to school. Pulling a kitchen chair up to the living room window, I aligned my knees with the metal ribs of the radiator. I propped my elbows on the windowsill and stared out. Cars streamed past on High Street, headlights splintering into strange shapes through the lace curtains. She would come. Traffic thinned as eight, nine, and then ten o'clock rolled around. With every approaching car, my chin popped up, my face brushed the curtain, and I peered down at the road. One of these cars would make a left and pull into the driveway. I didn't even need a blinker, just a swift turn to say, "I'm home."

If we wanted something badly enough, Mom always said it would happen. How soon we found her, I knew, would be directly proportional to how hard we searched and how earnestly we waited. I didn't get up for dinner, and I didn't get up to go to the bathroom. Chris woke me a few hours later. My eyes snapped open. It was well past midnight and there wasn't a car in sight.

Chapter Three

THE NEXT MORNING I jumped out of bed and rushed back to the window, looking down to the driveway at the spot where her car was supposed to be. Already awake, Chris was sifting through the mail while Brad again checked for credit card activity. I started scraping my thumbs with my index fingers. Whenever I was stressed, I'd absentmindedly pick off the skin around my fingernails until blood appeared. My mom had the same bad habit, although she could usually stop herself before bleeding. After three days without her, my hands were as hacked up and bloody as they'd ever been.

All the friends and relatives who'd assured us that our mother had gone away for the weekend were mistaken. Saturday and then Sunday had passed without her return. For the first time I realized I couldn't even begin to fix what was wrong or pretend that it was okay. I was lost.

"We have to go to the police," Chris said.

I knew he was right—seventy-two hours had passed from when our mother failed to show up for work—but taking our worries to the cops was a last resort that seemed more fitting for an after-school special. Her absence would suddenly become official, known, broadcast. But we'd run out of other options.

Mom's apartment was only a five-minute drive from the Newburyport police station. Barbara Ann had driven over from North Andover, insisting that she come with us. Even though we were technically adults—all in our early twenties—I felt like my brothers and I were three little kids, adrift, and as we entered the station, I was grateful for Barbara Ann's maternal presence.

I'd been wearing my mom's sweatshirt since Friday. With a hull silhouetted on the front above the words WOODEN BOAT, the faded blue sweatshirt had been my dad's before Mom claimed it. The sleeves hung past my hands, making them convenient for wiping my runny nose and hiding my scabby thumbs.

We parked in the lot across from the two-story brick police station on Green Street, half a block from the waterfront boardwalk where we had hoped to spot our mom taking a stroll. Two granite steps took us into the lobby, empty but for us. I studied the purple rubber floor while Brad explained our situation to the officer at the front desk, stooping to speak through a fist-sized hole in a thick pane of glass.

The officer made a phone call and another policeman appeared as our escort. We followed him single file down the hallway and up a flight of stairs. I made tighter fists inside my sleeves as the officer knocked on a name-tagged door: INSPECTOR BRIAN BRUNAULT.

Brunault led us to a conference room adjacent to his office.

Chris, Brad, Barbara Ann, and I sat facing him across the table. He appeared to be about the same age as my mother. The inspector lacked the grizzled chain-smoking detective look I'd envisioned and instead had wavy blond hair, round glasses perched atop a knobby nose, and bright greenish eyes. He wore a tie and a button-down shirt with the sleeves rolled up; his police badge was affixed to the belt loops of his khakis. Inspector Brunault looked like a man who got things done.

But I couldn't look him in the eye. I was convinced that he was taking mental notes on us, sizing up our characters, quantifying just how badly we wanted our mother back. I avoided Brunault's gaze by studying the windowsill, which was lined with three colorful pipes, similar to the one I had stashed in my desk drawer back at school. Confiscated goods, I figured. I looked at my lap instead. Brunault would get suspicious if he caught me staring.

"Who was the last person to hear from your mother?" he began.

"I talked to her right before her phone shut off Thursday night," Chris said.

"What'd you talk about?"

"I asked how her day was. She was quieter than usual, but I figured she was just tired. Said she'd call tomorrow and hung up."

"Quieter than usual?"

"She usually asks us a ton of questions, about our day and work and school. But she seemed distracted."

"How long was the conversation?"

"A minute or two."

"And no word since?"

"No."

"So she went to work on Thursday. What does she do?"

"She works with handicapped students at the Greater Law-
rence Educational Collaborative."

"Have you spoken to her boss or anyone she works with?"

"Yeah. They couldn't remember anything out of the ordinary
on Thursday."

We gave him the phone numbers of our mother's boss and a
few colleagues. More questions ensued, but I stopped listening.
I wanted to be out searching for answers, not sitting in an office
repeating the few things we already knew. More than seventy-two
hours had passed, so where were the sirens, and what of the search
parties? Brunault was asking about suspects and possible motives,
opening my mother's disappearance to a realm of possibilities I
hadn't dared to consider. *Motives for what?*

"No, she didn't have any enemies," Brad was saying.

Sitting face-to-face with an officer of the law was far worse
than calling friends and relatives to ask about our mom's whereabouts. Our friends and family understood how close we were and
how reliable she'd always been. But with a stranger outfitted in a
badge and a gun, everything was different. Our task was to convince him of a bond that we'd never had to put into words before,
to define a relationship we'd never had to question. Our legs were
shaking under the table. Tired and in need of showers, we were
forced to swallow our pride in a small-town police office, saying,
"There wasn't really a specific moment when things went wrong."

Brunault asked us to describe our mother's appearance. Brad
slid her work badge across the table, saying, "It's all we could find."
The lanyard snaked behind. Dug up from her purse, the only
recent photograph we had of our mother was from a laminated

and scratched ID. She wore turquoise earrings and a silver neck-lace. The photo looked like it'd been hastily snapped in front of a background of cubicles at her office, but it showed a kind face softened by freckles, laugh lines, and crow's feet. It was only a head shot, but we told Brunault that our mom was five-four and not exactly thin anymore. I wanted to tell him that getting her figure back was all part of her starting-over plan, but Brad was the one doing the talking. I knew it would come out sounding like a dumb girl comment, so I kept my mouth shut.

We got up from the table and Brunault walked us to the door, spouting off police jargon. "Statewide alert" was all I caught. The visit reminded me of going to the doctor, when I knew I needed to listen carefully and inevitably ended up forgetting most of the important parts. Although Brunault seemed eager to help us, it was unclear to me exactly what the police were going to do. I would have to ask my brothers to fill me in later, as if I hadn't been sitting right beside them as the inspector went over the procedure for issuing a statewide alert, obtaining a subpoena for our mother's E-Z Pass information, check-ing local hospitals, tracing bank accounts, and doing whatever else the police did when a person officially disappeared.

Chris and I waited in the hall while Brad and Barbara Ann spoke to Brunault for a few more minutes. Once outside, we thanked Barbara Ann for coming and promised to call if we needed anything.

My brothers and I got back in the Explorer and headed for Plum Island.

"That was weird," I said.

No one bothered to answer.

Chris drove slowly enough for us to keep an eye on the sidewalks while also peering down every passing side street. It was like being separated in the supermarket, running along the registers and looking down the aisles—cereal, baking supplies, canned foods—while shouting a name. I sat in the middle backseat, my hands pressed palm to palm between my knees. Brunault was not going to make an announcement for our mother to meet us at the front of the store.

Driving toward the island, we passed a whitewashed single-story house perched on a scrap of land that looked as if it were about to be swallowed by the encroaching harbor. Beach grass sprouted around the foundation. Fearing the tiny house's imminent collapse, I doubted whether anyone actually lived inside.

Such a classic New England coastal scene would compel our mom to stop the car, grab her camera from the trunk, and shoot an entire roll of film, adjusting the aperture and shutter speed until she got the perfect balance of light on the clapboard and blue in the background. She was always taking pictures yet never called herself a photographer. I'd tried to convince her more than once to make a career of it, but she shrugged it off as if it were an impossible dream.

We drove on in silence. Passing the turn for the wildlife sanctuary, I didn't bother to tell my brothers how Barbara Ann and I had almost ended up in the brackish water two days before. We made a right onto a narrow lane lined with beach houses. The island's homeowners often built upon stilts in an effort to protect their properties from hurricane flooding. With their spindly legs, the houses had a strange birdlike quality, as if they were just resting their wings for a while and never meant for this to be permanent.

The road ended in an empty beach parking lot. We walked through the dunes and down to the shore. The wind hurtled through our coats. We were the only idiots on the beach. The chance of being in the same place at the same time as our mother was infinitesimal, even if all we were doing was looping between the spots we thought she might be. We were spinning circles around each other, traversing a Venn diagram whose overlapping center was maddeningly out of reach. I wanted a voice mail of breaking waves, a clue to lead us home to her.

We walked back toward the parking lot, each of us lost in our own quiet disappointment. A black rubber glove was stuck atop a fence post bordering the path through the dunes. I envisioned my mom taking a photo of it, amused by the way the glove's fingers waved lazily in the wind.

The day after we filed the missing person report, my family decided that it was time for me to go back to school. According to my father, classes would be a good distraction. All we were doing was waiting—waiting for the police to stumble upon a lead, waiting to spot our mom, waiting for her to come home. I didn't want to wait by myself back in Rhode Island, but my brothers and I were starting to snap at each other. I couldn't see that they were trying to shield me from our wide-awake nightmare by giving me my daily routine back. I just thought they were trying to get rid of me.

My dad drove me to Providence on Tuesday afternoon. I stared out the window, refusing to speak to the man who had divorced my favorite person. I wanted someone to blame, and I'd always chosen my mom's team over my dad's (except during the Wiffle ball games of my youth, when Dad deemed me his "secret weapon," us against the boys, us against the world). I refused to acknowledge how helpful he had been since Saturday, when upon realizing that our mother really was missing, he began looking and calling various places nonstop, suggesting locations from their shared past, before the divorce and its attendant bitterness. Mom often said that Dad had ruined her life. Hers had seemed a good enough life to me, with a steady job, three kids, and a few close friends, but maybe there was more to it than I knew. Maybe the divorce had damaged her in ways I was too young to understand.

I waited for my dad to say the wrong thing so I could snap at him. We fell into a familiar uncomfortable silence; I looked for white Subarus on the highway. And then we were exiting, crossing the Providence River and climbing the steep hill of Waterman Street, approaching the dorms. I was about to be cut loose from my family, which struck me as the worst possible scenario. We idled at the curb, my dorm lit like a leering jack-o'-lantern. I wanted to say, "I talked to her every single day." I wanted to say, "I bet you wish you were a little nicer to her, don't you?" But mostly I wanted my dad to acknowledge that my mom disappearing was not the same as his ex-wife disappearing, even if we were talking about the same person. I assumed that my dad couldn't possibly care about my mom's well-being as much as I did, based on the fact that he had divorced her, while I'd remained her best friend and faithful daughter through all of it. That she was still the mother of his three children was not a vantage point I could see from. I fumbled for the door latch while he gave me a hug.

Back in the dorm, Cassidy unpacked my bag and asked if I was hungry or if I wanted to watch a movie. For a moment, I was just a sophomore in college, coming back to campus after a long weekend away. I was relieved to be lying on the floor with my best friend, but then the day count crept back into my consciousness. Five days. Five days my mother had been missing, and there I was, watching a movie.

I showered, dressed, and went to class on Wednesday. I'd promised my dad that I would go through the motions. Both of my parents had been proud to give my brothers and me a good education, splitting the costs of three pricey college tuitions between them. We'd had paper routes since we were kids and summer jobs since we were sixteen, but I didn't realize how lucky my brothers and I were not to have to worry about student loans. Dad often said that our mom spoiled us and made us unappreciative. He was the one living in a beachfront mansion, but he was also the one eating from economy packs of Cheerios and cans of Campbell's soup every day. Mom was more interested in taking us on trips and never saying no to our requests. I knew she spoiled us, but I figured Dad balanced things out by enlisting our help with his home-improvement projects every other weekend.

Dad had paid his Princeton tuition himself, scraping together summer earnings to cover the difference from his financial aid. Mom hadn't been able to afford room and board, and instead lived at home in Wellesley while commuting to Boston College. She wanted more for my brothers and me, while he wanted to make sure we knew just how good we had it.

Although I couldn't seem to convince my dad, I was grateful to be at Brown, and I never skipped class. I didn't know where my mother was, but at least she would know where I was. I'd show my dad too—pleasing them both, just as I'd been trying to do my whole life.

Except for one professor whom I knew well, I couldn't bring

myself to immediately tell my teachers what was going on and instead attempted to pretend that everything was normal. Wednesday afternoon I sat waiting for my poetry workshop to begin, scribbling eyes in the margins of my notebook. The last book I'd been reading was *The Unbearable Lightness of Being,* and the last thing I'd written before she disappeared was a phrase from the beginning:

The myth of eternal return.

And below that, my angry musings in jagged pen in the six days since everything had changed:

This isn't supposed to happen to us. Don't leave me, Mom.

Waiting for my professor to show up, I thought about how my mother had urged me to take an economics class instead of a "useless" poetry workshop the last time I'd called asking for spending money. I got a job making pizzas and stuck with the poetry. Since I'd started writing stories in high school, Mom had encouraged me, casting aside the more practical-minded instincts of my dad and brothers. But maybe she was right to finally call it useless, sounding for once like my father, who often said that I was pursuing a career in poverty: sooner or later I would have to give up my frivolous writing courses and get serious. Study business like my brothers. Learn something stable, a nine-to-five moneymaker.

Class started five minutes late. How much farther away could my mother get in five minutes? Continents, it seemed, because I was not out searching for her.

The student beside me read aloud a poem about Chanel lipstick. I couldn't offer any feedback on what my professor called a "subtle critique on capitalism," and because I didn't know how to segue from a lipstick poem to a missing person, I got up and walked out.

I wandered around campus for a while, called both my brothers, and reached both of their voice mails. Maybe they were on the other line with Mom. Maybe they were racing to pick her up at that very moment. Maybe they were having another powwow with Brunault. I hated my brothers for not answering their phones on the first ring. Hated my mother for six whole days gone straight to voice mail. Hated that girl for her dumb poem about lipstick. Hated everything all the way to the liquor store—everything except my fake ID, which would serve me well in the next nine months that I was still underage.

Back in my dorm, I yanked down the shades and topped off my glass with the Smirnoff I'd just bought. Cassidy had class and club lacrosse practice all day, and I had our room to myself for long enough to get drunk. By seven or so, the quad was getting noisy. Wednesday was a big party night at Brown, and our dorm was wedged between the fraternities. Just as I could feel the vodka warming me up and numbing me out, a voice came over a megaphone so loud that it seemed to be coming from right outside my door. But I knew, even before I looked, that it was some guy from the frat house next door, bellowing from the giant picnic table on their porch, most likely with a beer in hand. He cordially invited the entire quad to watch his fraternity's pledging freshmen strip naked and run through campus.

Windows opened and faces emerged. Snoop Dogg's "Gin and Juice" spilled out of nearby speakers. Onlookers cheered. Pale boys sprinted in the moonlight, whooping and holding their crotches in the hopes of becoming brothers. I shut the window. A few more days, I reminded myself, and then my banishment would be over. My spring break began the following week, which meant I would soon be back in the game, searching. With any luck, Mom would be home by then. But a few days suddenly seemed like a very long time.

I called my brothers obsessively. They didn't answer. I started to think that maybe I really had been discarded. Maybe my brothers blamed me, as I kept blaming myself, for our mom's disappearance, which I saw as a direct result of the argument we'd had on New Year's Eve. Maybe I did belong back at school, alone with my guilt. So much was built upon maybes. Brad finally called me back, saying they were busy before, and this was the first time he could call, and was I doing okay?

"Where were you?" I asked.

"We had an interview with Channel Five."

"The news station? Whose idea was that?"

"Brunault's."

"What'd you say?"

"We described her car. Gave the phone number of the police. Asked viewers to report any info."

"When will it be on TV?"

"Tonight at eleven."

"Thanks so much for including me. I'll just watch along with the rest of New England."

"Lindsay—"

I hung up. Really I was relieved. I wasn't newsworthy. I'd be too emotional. My brothers would be great. Implore thousands of viewers with their big dark eyes. For the first time in a week, they would be wearing clean clothes, button-downs and khakis, their faces freshly shaved. Who wouldn't want to help such hopeful and handsome young men find their mother? I called Brad back and apologized for hanging up.

"Mom wouldn't want you to miss school," he responded to my rant about being left out.

"Then why don't you go back to Cornell?" I asked.

"I can't."

"Fine, I'll call you after I watch it."

What were the chances that Mom would watch the news, register our concern, and come home? Except she wouldn't see me, because I wasn't there, which would mean that I didn't care as much as my brothers. I worried about this and called her phone repeatedly until just before eleven, on the slim chance that she would answer and we could cancel the newscast. But it kept going to her voice mail, which was already so full of messages that I couldn't leave another.

I didn't have a TV, so I went downstairs to my friend Andrew's room to watch. We flipped through the stations only to find that Channel Five didn't air as far south as Providence, or maybe it was that he didn't have cable. Either way, eleven o'clock came and went. We kept channel surfing, thinking we might have missed it. All I wanted was to see how my brothers looked on TV, mouthing the words, "Our mother is missing." But maybe it was better that I never saw.

The police did not receive the immediate slew of tips they were hoping for in the wake of the newscast. Our phones, however, rang off the hook. Family friends and acquaintances—some so distant they had to remind us how we knew them—called to say they were shocked to see us on TV. Did we need anything? A home-cooked meal or an extra set of hands? Everyone wanted to tell us about the last time they had been with our mom and how routine it had been. We said thanks because we couldn't say they were making it worse. Mom raised us not to air our dirty laundry, and now it was out on the line for all of New England to see.

Before I grew to dread the sympathy calls, I lunged for the phone when I didn't recognize the number of an incoming call. Split-second fantasies passed through my mind: Mom calling from Bermuda, from a beach, from a boat, from a hotel, from right outside my dorm, from anywhere. I would try to remain calm on the line because the police had warned us that she might be disoriented, but just hearing her voice would be ecstasy.

With no credit card activity and no sightings of our mother's car, the police soon ran out of information to work with. Ours was a "lead-driven case" without any leads. Brunault had shut down other cases at the department, putting his whole team on the search. Mom had an entire police department baffled.

We were still waiting on the subpoena for her E-Z Pass records. The more time passed, the less relevant tollbooths seemed. Even if Mom had driven to New Hampshire on Thursday night and paid the tolls, she could be clear into Canada by this point. She could be anywhere by now, and anywhere was too big an area to search.

I stayed busy at school studying the effects of various substances. Red wine and sleeping pills held the nightmares at bay. Vodka gave me hiccups. Beer was like water. I drank whatever I could get my hands on, downing various pills with my booze. It didn't matter what the capsules contained, only what they could suppress.

A year earlier, the school psychiatrist had prescribed me Prozac. The feelings I'd described struck him more as depression than standard freshman homesickness. Initially the Prozac had helped, and I was adjusting to living away for the first time. By the fall of my sophomore year, I was actually enjoying Brown and starting to create a life apart from my mother's, a life of my own. But then March 17 happened.

Suddenly there was a new urgency to my pill use, and the innocent-looking blue-and-white capsules became a convenient method of checking out. I decided to double my 20 milligram dosage. Even at the lower dosage, I'd been able to get tipsy from one glass of wine, but I couldn't stop at one any more than I could figure out where the hell my mom had gone. Combining liquor with antidepressants was like being out at sea, in the dark, the whole boat rocking and my body just trying to find the rhythm of the sway.

My college friends sensed that something was wrong, but I was too proud to tell the full story to anyone other than Cassidy. I was ashamed to talk about the news, the police, the sleeplessness, or the crazy theories consuming my thoughts. Really, I was just as private as my mother, and I'd become defensive and unapproachable in my disheveled state. I was taking most of my meals in bed, emerging from my dorm room only to go to the communal bathroom down the hall. Friends dropped off plastic bags full of weed and envelopes containing unmarked pills. I smoked or swallowed their offerings, grateful for the release.

But when the buzz wore off, one sentence thrummed along with the hangover headache: *My mom is missing.* If this was my new reality, I wanted no part of it. I operated on some combination of Prozac, liquor, and pot as often as I could. Despite my extracurricular activities, somehow I was still turning in papers and other assignments. It might not have been my best work, but at least I was keeping my head above water.

Chapter Four

THE DAY AFTER the news aired, Brad called to tell me about the flyers. We had hoped it wouldn't be necessary to paste a photo of our mother on every telephone pole and tree in town. But six days had passed: almost an entire week, too long to be lost.

"Which photo?" I asked.

"The one from her work badge."

It was a decent head shot. But still, I didn't like knowing that we were using the photo from her work ID because it was the only one we could find. As much as she loved taking pictures, Mom hated having her own picture taken.

"Chris and I are going to hang a bunch. I'll e-mail you one."

"Okay."

I hung up the phone, ran to the bathroom, and crouched over the toilet, heaving. I pictured my mother driving home from a trip that would make perfect sense once she had a chance to explain herself. Exiting the highway and driving through town, she would pass a tree with something stuck to it. She might not look too closely. It might not be until the next intersection, idling at a red light and looking around, that she would see another flyer, taped to a telephone pole beside the road. The face would look familiar. A split second later she would register the features as her own, on a flyer declaring her missing, like a runaway cat. I could see her cheeks turning red, could hear her heart pounding. If speaking openly of divorce or therapy shamed her—I had learned the hard way about a wide range of subjects I was not to mention to friends—then I had a feeling she would view this poster as the ultimate mortification. If Mom came home, she was going to kill us.

The newscaster at least had the decency to bookend our tragedy with sports and weather, shepherding viewers from football to a missing person to partly sunny skies with a chance of afternoon showers. You could change the channel or shut it off altogether. But a face taped to a pole had a way of lingering.

My mother's face.

My breath quickened. I threw up a little. My forearms rested on the cool porcelain as my breath ran raspy. I stayed in the stall, spinning the toilet-paper roll and quietly weeping.

Back in my room a few minutes later, I opened my e-mail and studied the face from the ID that we had slid across the table to Brunault a few days earlier. It felt like years had passed since. The contrast was heightened in black and white, my mother's chin-length brown hair becoming a black frame around her face. Her turquoise earrings held the curve of question marks, and the silver chain around her neck featured a heart pendant that I hadn't noticed before. Stripped of their green-yellow flecks, her eyes looked small and beady. Her teeth were extra white, smiling out between two dark stripes of lipstick.

MISSING marched across the page above her face. I couldn't decide whether the bold capital letters conveyed desperation or determination. I needed to believe that the flyer would help us find our mother, but like going to the police, it served to heighten my alarm at how serious our situation had become.

I wanted to ask my brothers why we weren't offering a reward, but it was impossible to say how much money a sighting would be worth. Any amount would make us seem crass. Too little would mean we didn't want her back badly enough, but too much would prompt false sightings from people looking to cash in on our uncertainty. It was safer to skip the reward altogether and rely on the simple belief that people were good, people would help.

My brothers hung the first round of flyers around Newburyport while I stayed in Providence. I took the train home again on Friday, March 24: spring break. I spent the next few days driving around with Chris, relieved that we had something to do, a definite purpose that kept us from pacing Mom's apartment. Brad was off on separate search missions much of the time, meeting with the police or manning the apartment while Chris and I went out. The three of us papered hundreds of gas stations, drive-thrus, and stores around Massachusetts, Rhode Island, and New Hampshire. Hanging flyers followed a relatively simple formula: stop, speak, fumble, hang, and go.

"My mother is missing, can I hang this here?" I'd begin.

The more I said this, the faster it came out, until it became one long word. My request was usually met with a few moments of thick-swallowing silence and downcast eyes. Then I'd fumble with the tape until the gas station owners or clerks would say, "Go right ahead," as if their mouths were just catching up with their brains. Perhaps for a moment they'd imagined what it would be like to have their own mothers disappear. They always said yes.

I could feel them watching as I positioned the flyers and pulled at the tape. The scabs on my thumbs kept splitting. It was still cold enough for gloves, but gloves were too clumsy for the job. Clawing at the edge of the packing tape demanded precision. By this time, all ten of my fingers were picked open and bloody; two thumbs no longer provided enough relief. Finding the edge on Scotch tape would have been quicker, but I needed something stronger to ensure that the flyers wouldn't be ripped down anytime soon.

One hanging deviated from the pattern. Chris and I were in Jackson, New Hampshire, checking the roads between our mother's new house and the surrounding mountains. We pulled into a gas station adjacent to a discount mattress store. A strange combination, but this was New Hampshire—the only state with liquor outlets along the highway, state-operated and tax-free. I took a flyer and walked into the mattress store while Chris went into the Quick-Pick. I had my line down, so many times said, and never once questioned:

"MymotherismissingcanIhangthishere?"

The owner of the mattress store straddled the corner of a bed as though he had just woken from a midday nap. A tag to his right read BOX SPRING AND MATTRESS ONLY $299! The store was empty but for us. I asked my question to his scuffed loafers. He squinted at the photo and stroked his beard in a look of dawning recognition. My eyes darted around the store. And then the mattress man was saying he'd seen the story on the news, and it was really something, and everyone up here was talking about it, and God it must be horrible, and had we received any sightings yet? I was unprepared for this, more of a hit-and-run hanger, too exhausted to play the victim or fan the curiosity of strangers. The man was practically bouncing on the bed. I stood frozen with my flyer, wary of questions and hungry only for answers. Just when I thought he was about to start up again, Chris rushed in and said, "Let's go." I was taking longer than the requisite minute. My brother ushered me out the door as the man rose from the bed and said, "Wait—hang a flyer here!"

From the mattress store, Chris and I went to our mother's new house. This was the first time I'd seen it. Nestled down a hill from the main road, the yard opened to a valley at the foot of the White Mountains. Acres of trails stretched out in the distance, places for my mother to hike, take photographs, and live "more simply," as she kept saying.

The house was yellow with a green tin roof above a wraparound porch. It was quaint and way too big for one person. We walked in the door and I instantly knew she hadn't been there. I was like a dog yearning to sniff out her scent. But even as I sensed she was elsewhere, I walked through the house struck by how much it suited her, with its lofted ceilings, side-by-side bathtubs, and wood cookstove. Cozy and rustic: the way I pictured retired life, with plenty of room for my brothers and me to come visit. We left a note for her on the kitchen counter, asking her to call us. She'd been gone a little over a week. Chris and I got back in the car and resumed our rounds, stopping at gas stations, post offices, and country stores, taping flyers of her face to doors and windows.

Days after it would have been most useful, the police obtained our mother's E-Z Pass toll records. Even an expedited subpoena took time, time we did not have. Finally, a week and a half after her disappearance, E-Z Pass yielded the one clue we hoped would give us some definite answers. The transponder printout recorded our mother traveling north through the Hampton tolls at nine forty p.m. on Thursday, March 16, two hours after she had talked to Chris and turned her phone off the night before she'd failed to show up for work. Hampton was the first of three tolls on our usual route to New Hampshire. The tollbooth deduction confirmed our initial assumption that Mom had gone to North Conway for a long weekend.

But the E-Z Pass record also showed her traveling through the same toll forty-five minutes later. Heading south. There was nothing but a long stretch of interstate on either side of the Hampton tolls. For some reason she had turned around halfway into the two-hour drive to her new house. Had she gotten spooked at the thought of being there alone? Our one promising clue took us north and then south, erasing its tracks and leaving us more confused than ever.

Without any more clues to follow, and without a decent night's sleep in more than a week, my brothers and I retreated even further into our private spheres of dread. We paced the apartment hoping Mom would walk in the door, but as the days crept toward April, it sank in that our ending would not be as easy as that. Silence hung between us whenever we were together. When we split up on separate search missions, we called each other incessantly, checking in and reporting on the lack of news. Discussing our fears was useless. The Harrison way had always been to keep your chin up and deal with whatever came next.

I blamed the lack of swift resolution on the police, declaring them lazy amateurs who had never solved a real crime in their sleepy brick-and-cobblestone town. I didn't realize the heroic efforts Inspector Brunault and his team were making to find my mother: repeatedly checking in with other police departments, keeping the alert status active in New Hampshire, reading patient lists at hospitals, and following up on recycled hunches and clues. It was not enough. Nothing would be enough until they found my mom and brought her back to me.

My father also made a convenient scapegoat. I reasoned that he couldn't possibly be as worried as I was, seeing as I loved this woman above all else, and he'd long ago fallen out of love with her. Letting Dad into the inner circle of our search party would mean breaking down all the barriers my mother had so carefully constructed between us and our father growing up. If he were the one to find her, she would probably keep running the other way. Despite Dad's repeated offers to help hang flyers and speak to the police, my brothers and I needed to do these things on our own. We used his house as a crash pad on nights when our mom's apartment felt almost haunted.

This new phase of stagnancy propelled us toward theories that seemed more and more unlikely, asking each other multiple times a day *what if?*

What if our mother had been abducted? We couldn't fathom

why someone would want to take her, but still. Her passivity in this theory was comforting. Should we be looking for a ransom note along with the growing pile of unpaid bills in her mail?

What if Mom had harmed herself in some way? What if she decided that life wasn't worth living anymore and had done something irreversible? This was the easiest theory to dismiss. There was no way that our mother would abandon my brothers and me by committing suicide. We were her whole life; she wouldn't do that to us. Besides, she had so much to live for—upcoming retirement, a new house in the mountains and a new simpler lifestyle to go with it. Aside from high blood pressure and some extra weight, she was mostly healthy. And other than being a little isolated in Newburyport, she was mostly happy. Close to her kids, money in the bank, a future in the mountains: hers was a good life, and it was downright impossible that she would throw it all away. Even if she were upset about something I didn't know of, she'd get through it, just like she'd always done. Her father's sudden death, her bitter divorce, and her mother's decline in a nursing home—our mom had walked through these trials with a tough New England self-sufficiency that was as fail-safe and reliable as it was closed off and proud. She was a fighter.

What if Mom had been murdered? The victim of a random crime? And what about Peter? We started to think it more than coincidence that our next-door neighbor from North Andover happened to move into the apartment across the hall from Mom's place in Newburyport a few months after she did. Hadn't they gone out to dinner back in the fall? As far as I knew, it had been Mom's only date since her divorce from our father almost two decades earlier. I never asked her why she hadn't sought romance in all that time—she'd probably have used the excuse of being too busy or not trusting men after my father—and it didn't strike me as odd, more as just the way it was. She was my mom, and I couldn't see her in any other light.

But she was excited to go out to dinner with Peter, and I remember her calling to ask me what shoes she should wear.

"Wear those green wedge sandals we bought at T.J.Maxx. Don't wear your sneakers," I said.

I'd phoned the next day to ask how the date had gone, and I racked my brain trying to remember what exactly my mother had said about this man who always seemed to be across the street. He was a little dull—was that what she had said? Or was it something more telling? Didn't he seem to thunder up the stairs and into his apartment a little too quickly? And when he came up the stairs slowly, it was because he was carrying his dog, and wasn't that also strange? Can't dogs climb stairs? And how about Peter's bespectacled eyes—weren't they a little shifty when we asked him if he had seen our mother recently? Didn't they bulge at the sight of the police leaving our apartment while he fumbled for his keys? And what of that pizza that he left on our doorstep as we crouched on the floor going over clues for the millionth time? He knocked and left his business card but was back inside his apartment by the time we got to the door. Were these the actions of a guilty man? I would like to say that I didn't eat any pizza from a man I imagined had murdered my mother, but I'd been hungry.

The police had questioned Peter within the first few days of the search. Brunault agreed that it was strange that he'd been our neighbor in North Andover and then Newburyport, but it was nothing more than random coincidence. Peter was just a well-dressed man who'd taken our mom out to dinner after his own wife had left him and he'd sold his house and rented a small apartment. A good neighbor. No one in the building had seen our mother or anyone else coming and going from her apartment around the time of her disappearance.

What if our mom had snapped? Was that just a saying, or could someone's mind literally snap? I could almost hear her dismissing this theory as ridiculous. According to my mother, most mental illnesses were "inventions born of self-pity." Only the weak and attention starved saw therapists. I was one of them and had earned this label firsthand. By the second week of the search, though, my brothers and I began to seriously consider whether there was more to our mother's life than we knew. What if, underneath that proud smile, Mom had a few screws loose?

After hours of reading about obscure mental illnesses on the Internet, we came across one condition that sounded all too fitting. The American Psychiatric Association's website defined dissociative fugue as follows:

1. Sudden unexpected travel away from home or one's customary place of work, with inability to recall one's past.
2. Confusion about personal identity or assumption of a new identity.
3. Significant distress or impairment.

Because many of these symptoms overlap with dementia, amnesia, and bipolar disorder, few cases of dissociative fugue have been diagnosed. The symptoms alone were enough to convince us, though. It was strangely comforting to think that our mother's disappearance was brought about not by a conscious act of will but rather by a betrayal of her own mind. Michele Harrison didn't drive away as our mother, as the owner of a new house, or as a teacher approaching retirement. She left as a woman without a name, without a past, and without a discernible destination.

The fugue theory meant that Mom hadn't left on purpose, making my guilt entirely beside the point. Her insanity absolved me; our New Year's Eve fight had nothing to do with it. Mom would snap back and remember once we found her, hugged her, kissed her. Identity would flow through her like good whiskey, burning for a moment before settling into the warm amber light of memory. She would chuckle in disbelief at how we'd been searching high and low for her. And we would laugh too, until the whole thing seemed a wild detective story on late-night cable. A fugue didn't demand forgiveness or recompense. Mom's disappearance was a big blameless mix-up, destined for nothing more or less than a happy ending.

But a fugue also meant that our mother probably wasn't going to come home on her own. Maybe she would recognize her face on a flyer or the news reports and jolt back to her old self. More likely, though, someone would see a lone wandering woman and recognize her from the news. They would call the Newburyport police and tell them exactly where to find her. We were ready to race anywhere. We sat by the phone and waited for a stranger to become our hero.

The first call came on Friday, March 24: two days after Channel Five had broadcast our story and a week after she'd disappeared.

I'd just arrived back at my mom's apartment for the start of my spring break, anxious to hang missing person flyers and crack the case myself. The police received a call from a man who claimed to have seen our mother in a bar in northern Maine, where he'd passed through on a snowmobiling trip. It was only after he got back to Massachusetts—he happened to live one town over from Newburyport—that he saw Chris and Brad on the news and reported the sighting. Despite this neighborly alignment of time and place, my brothers were skeptical. Where the hell was Millinocket, Maine, and what would our mom be doing in the Blue Ox Saloon on a Sunday night? Furthermore, how would she get up there without traveling through at least five tollbooths? We couldn't align this sighting with the E-Z Pass record, which last traced her heading south.

But desperation made any destination possible, and dissociative fugue made any place just as likely as the next. I resolved the tollbooth discrepancy by deciding that Mom must have chucked the transponder out the window for some reason. Or maybe she had taken the scenic route, weaving up the coast and avoiding the highway altogether.

After alerting the Millinocket police department, Inspector Brunault told us that we'd have to search the area ourselves, as it was out of his jurisdiction. Chris spread a map of New England on the floor of Mom's apartment and we traced the route she'd likely taken. Two hundred and seventy miles lay between Newburyport and Millinocket, more or less a straight shot up I-95. It was practically in Canada, this town so small we had to squint to see it. Our mom followed her routine as carefully as a tightrope walker: call her kids, go to work, visit her mother, walk on Plum

Island, eat dinner alone, call her kids again, go to sleep, wake up, repeat. So what was she doing so far from home, in a town pierced by the whinny of chain saws and snowmobiles? Dissociative fugue answered this question for us.

I assumed Chris, Brad, and I would hop in the Explorer and gun it for the north country. But we couldn't leave Newburyport unattended. What if Mom came back and we were out searching for her in a place she had only passed through, and days ago at that? Brad was the most levelheaded among us. He immediately started planning the trip while Chris and I made wild conjectures about what Mom could be doing in a run-down logging town in the woods of Maine. Hiking? Not likely at this time of year. A photography expedition? New Hampshire was her tireless subject for the camera. A fugue state—of course, she was just lost!

Because Brad was the first to learn of the disappearance, because Brad had been the bearer of bad news, and because Brad was the one in daily contact with Brunault, it was Brad who would get to find our mom. Unlike me, Brad remained composed under the worst of circumstances. I'd never once seen him cry, and dry eyes were the most suitable for searching. His best friend, Brodie—who knew our mom like his own—was leaving school and would meet Brad en route. When I asked if I could go, his response was not up for discussion.

"You're staying here," he said.

I didn't deserve to be the hero. I skulked to the fridge for another beer.

Brad got in his truck, a fat stack of flyers on the passenger seat. Chris and I stood in the silence that followed his tires on the driveway, the road, and the rumbling out of sight. What would we do without Brad telling us what to do? Would he call us every hour as promised? Call the second he found her, or even better, would he hand Mom the phone and let her say hello herself? What if she wasn't happy to see him? What if she didn't want to be found at all? We didn't dare try to answer the questions that kept seizing us.

Chris and I drove around Newburyport some more, turning our conversation back to blind speculations about what could have lured Mom to Millinocket in the first place. From what I understood about the fugue theory, even if you snapped and forgot your identity, you could still be pulled toward a significant location from your past. You might not know exactly why you were there, but it's not always about why—some places you just circle back to. We called friends and relatives and asked them what they knew of Millinocket. We were hoping that by placing the town within the context of her life, we could come up with some more places where she may have been drawn to. But none of her friends had ever been to Millinocket or heard our mother mention it.

We called our father and told him of the sighting.

"Millinocket? Never heard of it," he said.

"Are you sure?" I asked.

"I can't imagine why your mother would be up there."

We had already told Dad about our fugue theory, but kept our abduction and murder speculations to ourselves, since they became completely ridiculous when said aloud. Dad was far too rational to believe in fugues, though.

I hung up, enraged that my dad had never taken my mom on a romantic trip to northern Maine. Why couldn't his past align with our present needs? He had no more answers than we did, and I resented him for it.

Static and crackle. The farther north Brad drove, the worse his cell phone reception got. Chris kept shouting, "I can't hear you!" into the phone, because everything could have changed since the last time we'd spoken a whole twenty minutes earlier. Twenty minutes was an eternity; in truth, all it took was an instant, one phone call. But Brad was calling only to report on the frequency of MOOSE CROSSING signs along the highway. The metal warning signs outnumbered cars, exits, and lights.

"Can you imagine hitting one of those fuckers?" he bellowed into the phone.

Brad and Brodie sounded farther from civilization with every call. Brodie was like my third brother, overprotective and annoying. He and Brad had beaten up every one of my high school boyfriends, saying I was too good for them. He'd eaten dinner at our house on a regular basis and had been a fixture at our ski condo on winter vacations. My mom adored him.

Chris and I stayed at the apartment in Newburyport, waiting for our mother to return or for Brad to call. So much of searching was waiting. Brad checked in with us at midnight.

"What's going on?" I asked.

"The Blue Ox is a sketchy dive bar, not the kind of place Mom would go," Brad said.

"Did you talk to the bartender or anyone?"

"He didn't work Sunday. Not too friendly to outsiders up here. We drank a few beers and got out of there pretty quick. I can't see Mom going there by herself."

"Maybe she wasn't alone. What're you doing now?"

"Checking into a motel. We'll scout it out in the morning when we can actually see."

I'd been so sure that this saloon would lead us to our mother. But it was wild hope that made me believe in the Blue Ox sighting at all, and hope, I was learning, was not enough to bring back the missing.

Chris took the couch and gave me the bed again. Waiting for sleep was our least favorite part of the day. I began to wonder how much longer our prayers would go unanswered. Hoping for my mother's return was causing more paranoia, in a way, than her actual absence. I clasped my hands on my belly and made a short plea to God to find her. I'd taken to praying with extra fervor since March 17, although religion hadn't played much of a role in my life before then. Mom raised us Catholic, in that church-on-Christmas-and-Easter-only kind of way. The older we got, the more my brothers and I squirmed and embarrassed her in the pews at St. Michael's, and eventually we stopped making the twice-yearly masses altogether.

Dad was an atheist and said that religion was meant for people who couldn't find enough to believe in here on earth. It was hard to have faith in our current circumstances, though, and seemed an appropriate time to ask God for help. I interlocked my scabby fingers and considered whether he was likely to be listening, or whether it was like calling my mom's phone: straight to voice mail, God unavailable.

When Brad called the next morning, he reported on the seedy motel he and Brodie had stayed at: stray hairs on the sheets and indeterminate stains on the polyester blankets. I pictured my brother and his best friend falling fast for a few hours' sleep, not even bothering to take off their dirty jeans. And then rising as the first light of day came shafting through the vertical slats of the window blinds. Leaning over to double-knot their hiking boots before going out to the truck again, the cab's floor littered with Gatorade bottles and flyers.

But they got in the truck with a little more hope than the night before. After Brunault reported the sighting to the Millinocket police department, the video clip from Channel Five aired on several local stations throughout Maine, and two more sightings had surfaced during the night, tripling the chances of our mom actually being up there. Brad said he was going to talk to our latest potential heroes, a policeman and a nurse. Their sightings seemed more probable than Mom being at a bar on a Sunday night. Hundreds of miles south, Chris and I could hardly sit still, feeling so close to a happy ending and so far removed from the action of it. Between Brad's updates, we called Mom's cell phone, only to hear the ringing and the automated recording we'd heard hundreds of times already: "I'm sorry, but the person you are trying to reach is unavailable . . ."

Brad learned that a retired Millinocket policeman had been buying a pair of pants in the town's only department store on Monday, March 20, when he saw a woman wandering aimlessly through racks of clothing. He knew almost everyone in town and was quick to spot a stranger. He said hello and asked her how she was doing. She stared at him blankly before walking away.

If the American Psychiatric Association listed examples of people lost in fugue states, I was sure this was textbook worthy. Mom hated department stores and rarely treated herself to new clothes. If she needed something, she would be in and out in a few minutes, not wandering among men's pants. And she would normally say hello. If not overly friendly, she was at least always polite to strangers. I hated the thought of her weaving through a brightly lit department store, like a lost little kid whose parents would not be waiting at the register.

The day after that, a nurse reported seeing our mother's car in a parking lot. She recognized it because it was the same make and model as her own, a 2005 Subaru Outback, taking note of the unspoken bond between drivers of the same vehicle. She didn't remember seeing anyone in the car, although she was fairly certain about the green Massachusetts license plate. But what really made me believe the nurse—a good and trustworthy person by her profession alone—was what she said about the stickers. When she called to report the sighting, she mentioned the Brown and Cornell decals on the back window. How many white Subaru Outbacks could be driving around Millinocket with these two stickers on the trunk?

A bar, a department store, and a parking lot. If Mom was in Millinocket for three consecutive days, maybe she was still there. Brad and Brodie drove down every street, hanging flyers on telephone poles and trees, knocking on doors, and talking to the town's residents.

Millinocket was a blip among mountains. Mt. Katahdin, the northern tip of the Appalachian Trail, loomed blue-gray in the distance. Lakes abounded. From what Chris and I could glean from the Internet, it was a view our mother would appreciate. We called Brad and told him to check for lakefront cottages that might be available to rent. As usual, he was one step ahead of us and had already pressed the local police about this possibility. Chris flipped to Maine in our atlas and we immediately saw the problem for ourselves. The map key boasted of two hundred and fifty recorded lakes in the region.

"I just talked to the head of the Millinocket police force, real nice guy. Said there are logging roads out to the cabins. But all the snow's melting up here and they're muddy as shit. If we try, we'll get stuck," Brad said.

I waited for Brad to tell us the plan. Never mind our hope, despair, or wild theories; it was his faith that he would find our mother that was carrying him all across New England, and finally to the Canadian border, where he spent the next four days moving from one border crossing to the next, leaving a trail of flyers in his truck's throaty wake.

While Brad was driving along the edge of Canada without any luck, I was driving to the Newburyport post office. Our mother's mail had been another disappointing clue, torn open to reveal nothing but bills and coupons. Since we had little else to go on, I figured I might as well check it again, in case a ransom note or a postcard from a Caribbean isle was sitting in the PO box Mom rented in town. I was two blocks from the post office when blue lights started flashing behind me. I pulled over, knowing I couldn't possibly have been exceeding the speed limit since I'd been driving extra slow to check the sidewalks for my mother. The officer came to the window and pointed to the expired registration sticker on the windshield of my dad's old Chevy Suburban. He returned to his cruiser and wrote me a ticket, sauntering back up to the window ten minutes later.

"Do you know who I am?" I asked.

"Yes, ma'am," the officer said, flicking the ticket onto my lap.

"Then maybe you know that my mother has been missing for over a week."

"I'm well aware of the situation, ma'am. We're doing everything we can to help your family."

"But stopping people for expired stickers is a better use of your time and resources?"

"Just doing my job, ma'am. Your sticker's expired and that's a federal offense. Now move on before I have you towed."

"You've got to be kidding me."

"I'll be sure to pass your appreciation on to the department, ma'am," he said, walking back to his car.

I parked outside the post office. The tears came hot and fast, my body slumped over the steering wheel. It was the first time I'd really cried since she'd disappeared. It all came up. I was so tired, so scared, so alone. And I didn't like being called ma'am.

But crying was not going to bring her back. I wiped the tears from my cheeks, shredded the ticket, and got the mail: nothing but a monthly statement from Bank of America, revealing no recent debit card activity.

My brothers lit into me as soon as I got back to Dad's house, where Chris and I had been staying. Inspector Brunault had called to tell Brad about my "emotional outburst" that afternoon. Apparently I had offended the entire Newburyport police department. Exhausted on his drive back from Maine, Brad was less than thrilled to hear this. He called again.

"What the hell were you thinking?" he began.

"What was *he* thinking, giving me a ticket?" I said.

"It's his job!"

"His job is to find Mom!"

"You don't know anything, Lindsay. Do you realize you just made everything worse?"

"*I* made everything worse? Well maybe if Dad didn't have a shitty old expired car this wouldn't have happened!"

Dad had been sitting quietly on the couch, listening to us argue on speakerphone. Dark circles ringed his blue eyes.

"Lindsay, Brad's right," Dad said.

"Why is everyone taking the officer's side? Chris, do you hate me now too?" I asked, as the tears came hot for the second time that day. He was sitting on the couch next to Dad.

"No, but why can't you just act rationally?" Chris said.

"*Act rationally?* Mom is missing—what part of that is rational?" I shouted, collapsing onto the couch with my face in my hands.

"You're out of control. Your drinking, your outbursts, and you smoke pot, which just makes you a loser," Brad said and hung up.

It was official. I'd ruined everything. Dad demanded that I write an apology letter. He typed it up, and though I didn't agree with a word of it, I signed it and faxed it to the Newburyport police department that night:

Dear Officer,

I'm afraid that during our conversation today, I acted very inappropriately. For this I am truly sorry. The stress and trauma of this situation has been overwhelming on my family and me, but I recognize that my behavior was out of line today. You were just doing your job, and I know the department is doing everything in their power to solve our case. Please accept my deepest apologies for my emotional outburst.

Sincerely,

Lindsay Harrison

With an absence of police activity over the next few days, I started to believe that I had made a fatal mistake. If we didn't find Mom, it would be my fault. I had offended the police, who were obviously too petty to accept my apology—or they had put it through some sort of lie detector test, where the buzzers went wild at my insincerity—and were now withholding information from us. I wouldn't forgive me either.

I kept my head down and did whatever my brothers told me to do over the next few days. When they vented about the lack of credit card activity—"How could Mom still not have charged anything?"—I echoed their frustration. When they said, "We should call her phone again," I listened to the recording for the millionth time. When we drove around with more flyers, I hopped out to replace the ones the rain had ruined, not even mentioning the soggy clumps of paper or the way running ink obscured her face. It wasn't just because my brothers were annoyed with me that we didn't talk very much, but more because there was nothing left to say.

Brad and Brodie didn't find our mother in Maine. The sightings petered out, up there and elsewhere. Brad drove back to Cornell to catch up on all the schoolwork he'd been neglecting. Chris returned to his managerial job in Boston, driving to Newburyport every night to check Mom's apartment. Dad drove me back to Providence at the end of my spring break, which felt like nothing less than banishment. Life demanded that life move on; I watched the days crawl by with alarming regularity. Brad was right—I was a mess. Each minute was such a long tunnel, and yet it had been two weeks, and then three.

I was obsessed with the sightings. I rationalized every anomaly until I was sure my mother had gone to Millinocket. She was in a department store because she was in a fugue state. She was in Maine without E-Z Pass knowing because she'd thrown the white transponder out the window and paid with quarters. She was at the Blue Ox Saloon because it was one of the only places open on a Sunday night. She was at a cabin in the woods because civilization often annoyed her. I could tell you exactly why my mother was in Millinocket. The trouble was, I couldn't tell you why she had left or where she was heading next.

And when my theories failed me, I still had my fantasies.

We could start over!

Mom, I don't even like college all that much. I'd take your company to these pseudohippie intellectuals any day. Do you want to move to Millinocket—were you scouting real estate up there? Decided New Hampshire wasn't far enough off the beaten path? We could find a nice fixer-upper on a lake. We could do that, Mom. I'll drop out of school and move up there with you. We can escape Massachusetts and its strip-mall infestation, wealthy suburbs, and self-righteous Yankees. We'll chop firewood and plant tomatoes and whatever else will take to the soil just south of Canada. I won't even tell the boys. It can be our little secret. Is running away fun?

I wouldn't mind being missing if it meant being together again.

But fantasies never last. A sighting isn't solid. It's not a home; there's no foundation. It amounts to one person's memory versus another person's doubt. Would my mother be memorable from only a flyer? I wanted to think so, but mostly she just looked like the next fifty-three-year-old woman, gravity and gray hair slowly getting the best of her. She looked like any mom in her button-down shirt, blue jeans, and sneakers. Did she ever really go to Millinocket? It's not exactly a yes-or-no question. People think they see things. On desperate days when I needed something to believe in, I built a whole house out of the sightings. Beams and right angles, Sheetrock and certainty. But as the days dragged on and everyone else resumed their lives, I came to see Millinocket like one of those prefab houses: not built to last.

Chapter Five

AFTER A WEEK of hanging flyers and chasing false leads, I was back at school. Besides Cassidy, I didn't tell any of my friends how I'd spent my spring break. Taping flyers all over New England seemed a far cry from their trips to warm tropical beaches. The more I talked about the situation at home, the more terrifying it became, and part of me believed that college could remain a little world unto itself in which the only things to worry about were papers, tests, and what parties were happening that weekend. All of this seemed irrelevant to me now, but still, I wanted to believe that everyone around me would be so caught up in the college mirage that I could self-destruct unnoticed.

One night I opened my door to find the five other girls who lived on my floor sitting in the hallway. We were friends by proximity, looking out for each other in the way dorm neighbors do. I went to the bathroom, splashed cold water on my face, and walked back to my room. They were whispering in urgent tones in front of my door. My friend Kelley stood up.

"Linds, we're worried about how much you're drinking," she said.

"You don't have to talk about me like this."

"But we're worried—"

"You can go now. I'm fine."

I shoved my way into my room and closed the door. But I knew they were still there, still whispering, and I had trapped myself. I grabbed my keys and stepped over them once more, running down the stairs and out to the quad, yelling that they had better not follow me. I wished Cassidy were here to see this, to defend me and tell me they'd crossed the line. But she was in the library cramming for a biology exam.

I had grown up with Kelley in North Andover. She had dated Brad throughout high school and was practically part of our family. So it wasn't a huge surprise that she called my dad that night. He phoned the next morning to rant about the evils of alcohol, which only served to heighten my fury. Here he was, lecturing me on how to deal with my mom being missing, as if he felt even a fraction of what I was going through. My dad never drank, not even on holidays. As far as I knew, he'd never touched the stuff. I couldn't imagine not drinking at a time like this, and told him as much.

The search dragged on. After Millinocket, there were no new sightings. With little to report, Chris and Brad were calling less. Even though our mother had been missing for four long weeks, it seemed the world was moving on without us. We tried to find the people we'd been before, but we were strangers to our old selves.

April brought the first warm days of spring, and students lounged around campus as if it were a beach. Enjoying the weather felt like betrayal. I squinted into the harsh sun as if the sky should only pour buckets of rain until I found my mother.

Falling behind in my classes, I met with a dean and told her what was going on. She urged me to take off as much time as I needed, opt for incompletes in my classes, and finish my work the following semester. But the last thing I wanted was for anything else to be left in limbo. The dean agreed to e-mail my professors about a family emergency, granting me a few extra absences and more time on my assignments. I stepped out of her office knowing that I wouldn't follow through on her suggestion to meet with a counselor at psychological services. There was nothing anyone could say, short of, "We found your mother," that would make it all okay. Silence seemed the only language capable of keeping my mounting terror in check.

On days I could get myself to class, it came as a relief just to be sitting somewhere other than in a tangle of sheets on my flimsy mattress. I sat in the back row, clutched my stomach, and scribbled in my notebook. On every page I drew eyes: jagged lashed, huge pupiled, haunted eyes. When I could stop sketching long enough to hear even two minutes of what my professor was saying, the distraction was accompanied by a deluge of guilt. Thinking about my mother's absence was a vigil I constantly had to attend.

I was walking back to my dorm from class one afternoon when I ran into my friend Jason. He suggested we go skateboarding, saying it was sure to make me feel better. I'd already told him the basics: my mother was missing, and no, I didn't really want to talk about it.

"I guess so," I said.

Jason ran to his dorm to get his boards.

I was wearing the shoes I always wore that year, blue canvas slip-ons with raffia soles—not the best skateboarding shoes. In gym shorts and a thrift-store T-shirt, my hair tangled and greasy, I was about as put together as I was going to get. Showering or wearing real clothes required energy I didn't have. All of a sudden I wanted wheels beneath my feet, wanted to push and glide away from this little college scene. Never mind that I didn't know how to skateboard.

Jason offered me the longer board, saying it was easier to manage. He gave me a quick lesson around the quad, showing me how to bend into the turns and keep my center of gravity low.

"This is easy. Let's go off campus," I said.

"Okay, but go slow," he warned.

I wobbled down Benefit Street, my body light for the first time in four weeks. I glided through intersections, not caring if the cars stopped. I knew they would stop. Providence was a city of jaywalkers, all college kids crossing streets with cell phones pressed to their ears. I had left my phone on my bed. I no longer wanted to answer the instant one of my brothers called. It was never good news anymore. It wasn't even news. It was just phone calls to report the absence of news, and I didn't need to be reminded of how many days had passed without our mother's return.

Chris would call to say he was trying to stay positive. Brad would call to say the police were doing what they could. I would tell them both that I was hanging in there, staying busy. We said the things we thought we should say, lies that no one believed, but pretending somehow felt like what Mom would want. She always said she was doing great, no matter the truth.

Thirty-one days. A day and a month she'd been gone.

We glided on, Jason calling out for me to bend my knees more and work the turns. We passed Hope Street and headed away from campus, where the houses got a little shabbier and a rusty bridge loomed above a dirty river. I was doing fine, turning wide and smooth, my face angled up toward the sun, when a slight downhill got the better of me. I crested over a ridge and tried to hop off the board and run it out. But there was too much momentum. My body smacked the pavement as the skateboard sailed toward the river littered with abandoned television sets. Jason went after the board, but he circled back to me soon enough. Tiny stones were lodged in my palms but the real pain was between my right shoulder and elbow. I limped off the street and retched onto the scrappy grass along the sidewalk while Jason called an ambulance.

Tears shuddered out of me. Blood and dirt shimmered where the skin had been scraped off my shoulder. This was what it was supposed to feel like to have your mother missing, a sure and sudden dislocation. So often it was a more diffuse pain and a handful of pills to keep it that way.

At the hospital, a series of X-rays revealed that I'd fractured my upper arm bone. The doctor said it was a miracle that I hadn't dislocated my whole arm or broken my collarbone. He spoke of miracles as if wonders abounded amid sterility and procedure, as if my careless encounter with pavement deserved such a word. Find my mother, I wanted to say.

Jason sat down on the side of the bed and asked me what I wanted for dinner. He felt awful about my accident.

"A cheeseburger," I said.

I clenched my teeth as the nurse tested my range of motion, bending my elbow up and out.

"That's where it hurts," I said.

"A cheeseburger?" Jason said.

While I picked up my Vicodin prescription at the pharmacy, Jason ran to the nearby market and bought a hunk of beef and an electric grill. I told him burgers weren't really necessary, that I had granola bars in my room, but he didn't seem to hear me. We took a cab back to my dorm. Jason set the grill on the carpet and molded two thick patties in the palms of his slender hands. He placed them on the grill and pulled a bottle of Bubba's barbecue sauce out of the grocery bag. The meat started to sizzle, the fat collecting in the lip of the grill like rain in a gutter. Jason doused the buns in the thick amber sauce while I rattled out painkillers. My right arm was bound up in a cheap blue sling. It wasn't easy to maneuver such a sloppy mess left-handed, but I was suddenly ravenous, and I couldn't remember anything ever tasting better.

Cassidy wrote BADASS on my sling that night. I took it off more often than the doctor recommended, lifting my arm until I could really feel the fracture. Physical pain was a relief—it was a tangible result, at least. Over the next week, I got more sympathy for my skateboarding accident than anything else. The sling was a good conversation starter and the skateboarding accident was easy to explain, a straightforward fall, nothing but a second between my body and the asphalt.

As final exams approached, I tried to make myself care about schoolwork. I wondered if Brad was also falling behind in his classes, but something had lodged between us, and I couldn't bring myself to ask him. When he called I drilled him with more pressing questions: When was the last time he'd heard from Brunault? What were the police doing? Were there any new leads? I knew the answers to these questions, but still I asked.

I pictured Brad calling Brunault while walking to his business classes. How brief their conversations must have become, how dreaded and routine. I imagined him plodding across the footbridges that span the gorges of Ithaca, connecting Cornell's sprawling campus. His shaggy dark hair pushed back under a baseball cap, his cell phone pressed to his ear. Nets had been hung from both sides of the bridges after more than a few despairing students had jumped to the coursing water hundreds of feet below. But I bet my brother never even looked down.

The days were passing relentlessly. Finally one began with a bit of good news, completely unrelated to the crisis at hand. It was Wednesday, April 26. I answered my phone and was offered a job teaching photography, which, given everything that had transpired since March, I'd completely forgotten I'd even applied for. A month or so before my mom's disappearance, I'd decided that teaching photography at a summer camp in Maine sounded like a nice getaway. After the camp director called to offer me the position, I spent the afternoon thinking how much I'd like to tell my mom about the job. Everything I knew about photography I'd learned from her. When Mom came home, I knew she'd be excited for me. Maybe I'd turn down the position, though, and spend the summer with her instead. I could work closer to home and sleep on the air mattress in her apartment as I'd done the summer before. I ventured into the sun with takeout from the dining hall, eating a mess of salad, veggie burger, and sweet potato fries awkwardly with my left hand, since my right arm was still useless in the sling.

I went back to my dorm around seven. Cassidy was studying at her desk. I plopped down on my bed, sleepy from the sun and feeling better than I had in a while. I'd eaten a good, hearty meal and I hadn't even had a drink yet. I curled up in bed and closed my eyes. My phone started ringing. It was most likely Chris or Dad calling to gauge how tipsy I sounded. Brad hadn't mentioned my drinking since the police incident, when he'd branded me a selfish pot-smoking loser, closing the subject at that.

"Hello?"

"Lindsay baby, it's Georgy!"

My uncle George always offered up an animated greeting, and felt it his duty now, more than ever, to inject some pep into his voice. George was my mother's younger brother, her best friend, and her instant plumber every time our basement flooded. Later he would tell me how he'd experienced a massive panic attack on the chairlift of a ski mountain right before I'd called to tell him of my mom's disappearance.

"Hey, George, no news," I said.

"I went to a psychic today to see if she could figure anything out about Micheley."

I had trouble picturing my burly sailor of an uncle consulting a frail old lady draped in shawls. But we were different now,

I reminded myself. We were no longer too good for supernatural mediums; tracing lines on a palm could mean as much as the next clue.

"What'd she say?"

"She kept saying, 'Micheley's on the dark side.' And I says to her, 'Well, when's she coming back?' She clutched my palms and said she didn't know."

Goose bumps pricked my skin. My phone beeped; Brad was calling on the other line. George kept saying the same things over and over to make it sound like there was more information than there really was. Repetition was its own kind of hope. I would call Brad back. I tried to focus on what my uncle was saying, but then Brad called for the third time in a row. I told George I had to go and switched to the other line.

"Brad, I'll call you right back, okay?"

"No," Brad said.

"No?"

"Linds, I love you."

"Don't—"

"They found Mom's body."

"No."

"In the water."

I fell down.

"Diver."

My body folded on the linoleum floor.

"Car."

I wanted so badly to hurl the phone at the wall, but it kept making sounds.

"Body."

His voice had flatlined.

"A diver was checking moorings in Rockport Harbor when he saw something white on the bottom. It was her car," he was saying.

"No."

"Off the end of a pier."

I wanted to tell Brad to stop talking, but my voice had crawled out of me. He was saying that Chris and Dad were on their way to pick me up and that I shouldn't do anything until they got there.

Cassidy crouched beside me on the floor, holding one hand over her mouth and clutching my fingers with the other. I called my uncle back and said the unthinkable myself, tasting salt on my tongue.

"They found her body. In the water."

George was crying and I wasn't. I said sorry and hung up.

I shut off my phone. I knew my dad and brothers would keep calling, but I didn't want the details.

I left my phone on the floor and walked out the door. Cassidy was right beside me. Down the stairs, across the quad, through campus and away, passing no one we knew. There was nothing to say, other than *oh my God* and *off the end of a pier*. One phone call had changed everything. For forty days I'd been hoping for a phone call, but in all that time I'd refused to believe that finding my mother could mean finding her body. *Underwater.*

Ten minutes later we got to where we both seemed to know we were going, though neither of us mentioned it: Prospect Park. A little park on a side street, where we came for picnics, where others came for romantic strolls and the view of downtown Providence. But tonight we were the only ones around. I gripped the cold iron fence posts as the city opened below us. The park was built into a steep hillside and the drop was at least a hundred feet.

Downtown the traffic lit up red and office buildings flattened into squares of yellow. I stared for a long time at the apartments being built by the river, spotlights illuminating three giant steel skeletons. Cassidy and I sat down on a bench.

"It wasn't supposed to end like this," I said.

"I know."

"In the water, I mean."

"I can't believe it."

Some amount of time passed, the night got colder, and we walked back to wait for my dad and brother, kicking a soccer ball across the empty streets. We'd found it in the park.

We were sitting in front of our dorm when my dad pulled up. Cassidy put my bag in the trunk and held me for a long time, my face collapsing into the hood of her tattered sweatshirt.

"I can come with you," she said.

"No, but come soon."

I climbed into the backseat, felt Dad shift into first gear, and watched Cassidy recede into a small hooded figure on the sidewalk. The car turned toward the interstate. I stared at the back of Chris's head, trying to imagine what could be going through it.

Dad's profile revealed nothing: clenched jaw, straight Roman nose, eyes locked on the road ahead. Oncoming headlights swept over him, but even in the light, I couldn't figure out who he was in relation to the person we'd just lost.

He and Chris took turns spreading the news by cell phone for most of the two-hour drive back to Dad's house in Beverly Farms.

We had grown used to constantly being on the phone during the search, but these calls were an all new kind of awful.

Brad had just begun his long drive home from Cornell. Dad called him every twenty minutes to make sure he was okay, although he didn't seem to be saying much. I knew Brad couldn't be talking that whole time; if he was crying, Dad remained silent, unsure of what to say but afraid to hang up. Chris called relatives and friends, saying "Our mom's body was found." That phrase was already too much and no one had the heart to press for details. Chris didn't have to say *diver* or *pier* or *Rockport Harbor*. Dad reached back for my hand. He squeezed, hoping for some sign of life in return. I could see his calloused hand holding mine, but I couldn't feel a thing.

My stepmother, Michele, was in the kitchen when we got back. Maggie was already asleep, and I couldn't imagine what it would be like in the morning. She would be thrilled about the convergence of her older siblings, who usually came together only for birthdays and holidays. She was six years old. Dad and Michele had protected her from hearing any mention of the search over the past forty days.

Michele put the kettle on for tea, conspicuously keeping herself busy and avoiding our eyes. The tea was too hot to drink and the mugs too hot to hold. Finally she looked up.

"Sorry about your mom," she said.

It would be a thing we would hear a lot—"I'm sorry"—and I would never figure out exactly how to respond. Growing up, saying sorry had always been about absolving guilt. I thought about how I had begged my mom to forgive me on New Year's Day. How she had dropped me off at Dad's house with all my clothes in trash bags, saying, "Sorry isn't good enough." How I had seen her only two more times after that. Four months later, it seemed that everyone was sorry.

I grabbed my backpack and headed for the stairs. I dropped my bag on my bed and fished out my pill bottle. I cupped my hands under the bathroom faucet, washing down a fistful of Tylenol PM with a swig of tap water. The nights were harder to get through with my arm in the sling; I had to sleep on my back. I stepped out of my jeans and slid between the cool sheets, feeling grains of sand that always seemed to find their way up from the beach that bordered Dad's front yard.

I kept waking in a cold sweat. My mind churned, and it would be the same routine for months to come: a split second of grogginess before I remembered that my mother had drowned in the deep blue sea.

Early the next morning, I pulled myself out of bed. I couldn't lie there for one more second pretending that sleep might come my way. Showering required too much effort. I went downstairs without bothering to change out of the T-shirt and jeans I'd worn the day before. I sat between my brothers on the couch. I didn't know what time Brad had arrived, and I didn't ask. Dad offered to make breakfast but we weren't hungry. Michele had already left for work, which struck me as insensitive. Had I been able to see things from her point of view—her home suddenly filled with her husband's ex-wife's death—perhaps I could have empathized. But my mother's body had just been found, and there was no other point of view.

Maggie came downstairs in her pajamas and climbed onto my lap, nuzzling her blond head beneath my chin. I didn't know what Dad or Michele had told her, but she seemed to know that something wasn't right, and that the best thing to do in a time like that is to hold on tight. She didn't say a word. She had always been a little shy around Chris and Brad, but I knew her affection was for all of us. I hugged her until she had to get ready for school.

After Dad got back from dropping Maggie off, the phone began to ring nonstop, as if everyone had been waiting for the decency of eight o'clock before calling. Dad was the first one up whenever it rang. After several relatives had called, I could hear my dad telling another caller to hold on a minute.

"Who was your mother's dentist?" he came in and asked us.

"Why?" I asked.

"The police need her dental records to identify the body."

None of us knew the name of her dentist. We switched on the TV and turned up the volume. Chris remembered the name, got up to tell Dad, and came back to our hideout on the couch. We left the TV tuned to Dad's favorite show—*This Old House*—and watched the plaid-shirted host build an elaborate chest of drawers.

A state trooper was driving from our mother's dentist in North Andover to the coroner in Boston, where her body would be officially identified through dental records (teeth being among the last body parts to decay). There was never any doubt, though. The police had already told us that the license plates on the car matched, the E-Z Pass transponder was on the dashboard, and the Brown and Cornell decals were stuck to the rear window. Comparing her teeth with a set of X-rays was really just a formality, but at least my brothers and I wouldn't have to go to the morgue.

Even though I was spared the sight of her body, I couldn't help imagining what it would look like after six weeks submerged in fifty-degree water. Had her eyes been open that whole time? And her mouth? I wondered if I'd even recognize her. I wondered if I would want to.

An autopsy would be performed. In time I would read the results and find little comfort therein, find little I didn't already know and details I didn't want to know. Most of her organs, as the medical examiner put it, were *unremarkable. The kidneys are unremarkable externally and on cut sectioning. Endocrine system: unremarkable. Digestive system: unremarkable.* As I'd imagined, the skin showed *prominent wrinkling due to prolonged submersion.* Her lungs, though, were worth remarking on: her lungs were *wet and edematous.* The final diagnosis listed the cause of death as drowning, and the manner of death as undetermined. *Wet lungs.*

Mostly unremarkable, mostly indeterminable. Or: there was officially little to say and even less to understand regarding the decedent Michele V. Harrison.

I was glued to the couch, stuck between my brothers for hours that first day death became a reality. Our knees were almost touching, but I'd never felt farther away from them. We were shocked into silence, sickened by six weeks of hoping for a happy ending. And I knew, as we swam through our mother's wreckage, that it would take a long time to salvage anything worth talking about.

We were still on the couch at dinnertime. A pizza grew cold on the coffee table that Dad had built years ago, sanding and varnishing a hatch recovered from a World War Two cargo ship. It was the only piece of furniture he had kept after his divorce. I picked the olives off my uneaten slice and pulled my knees up to my chest.

All day we had avoided talking about the thing that was making it hard to breathe, eat, or do anything besides stare at the television. But we had to make arrangements, because that's what death requires of the living.

Dad shut the door between the family room and the kitchen. Maggie was home from school, and the conversation we were about to have was unfit for a first grader to overhear.

It was easy to agree on what we *didn't* want for our mom's memorial service. Funeral homes smelled funny. They were for the dignified departed, hands clasped and hair parted, wearing Sunday's best in an open casket. Unsuitable for an "accident" that many suspected was something else entirely. We didn't belong in a function hall either, renting a space where weddings and conferences took place. And a church was out of the question. If there were a God up there, he'd let me down hard; we were not about to sit, stand, and kneel before an altar of any kind. We settled on Dad's house as the location, which struck me as being just as sacrilegious as a church.

His house was a hundred years old and had been a boarding school since the 1970s. When Dad bought the place in the early nineties, the wooden floors were glued over with purple carpets, the fireplaces were boarded up, and a towering fire escape was attached to the front of the house. Dad took one look at that mother of all fixer-uppers, offered a much lower price than what the school was asking, and signed the deed.

Dad's house hardly fit in with the pristine estates that lined the rest of West Beach. My father soon became known as the eccentric do-it-yourselfer who was going to renovate all forty rooms of his house without any help at all. The yard featured his pickup truck, an old backhoe, and blue tarps laid out for his latest painting project. The inside was cluttered with tools and half-finished renovations.

So yes, Dad's house was large enough to accommodate the swell of guests that would come on Sunday, and yes, having a beach for a front yard was nice for a get-together, but still. Mom hated Dad. Was this a memorial, or revenge? I tried to ask as much, but Brad told me to stop being so immature.

"Whatever you guys want. Here or somewhere else, it's up to you," Dad said.

"Here," Chris said.

"Here," Brad seconded.

"Fine, I don't care," I said.

There was still the question of the body. Burial seemed the obvious answer to me.

"Maybe we can get a plot next to her dad's grave," I suggested.

"She wanted to be cremated," Brad said.

"How do you know?"

"She told me."

"When?"

"Doesn't matter."

Chris was going to call the newspaper about the obituary. Brad was going to make the cremation arrangements, and I was going to sit on the couch some more. Besides not knowing what she'd want for her funeral arrangements, I didn't understand how it came to be that we were arranging her funeral at all. How on earth had our mother ended up in the ocean?

On Friday morning, Chris, Brad, and I went to empty Mom's apartment in Newburyport, stopping on the way for coffee and trash bags. Her landlord would have given us as much time as we wanted to clear out her things. But we needed to get off the couch. Being busy made it easier not to think—that had been the illusion behind hanging so many flyers, anyway. Dad offered to help, but this task fell into the growing category of things my brothers and I had to do on our own.

There was so much stuff. Cookbooks and clothes and CDs and silverware. Half-melted candles and framed photographs. A black-and-white I'd taken the summer before, a church steeple obscured by raindrops on the camera lens. A tube of toothpaste, a half-empty bottle of shampoo. A bottle of dark red nail polish I'd used to paint my mother's toenails the summer before, blowing gently on her feet to dry the paint. We stood in the living room with a roll of trash bags. I hadn't bothered to wear my sling, thinking that a thing like this *should* hurt.

I started with the clothes, wanting to get the worst task over with first. I emptied my mom's dresser drawers onto the bed. Then there was the tiny overstuffed closet, coats and hangers jutting out at all angles. The pile on the bed grew until it toppled onto the floor, socks and sleeves everywhere. My brothers and I had an unspoken agreement not to donate our mother's clothes to Goodwill. Her shirts lingered with the smell of sweat, detergent, and Red Door perfume. Stray hairs clung to her fleece jacket.

Her denim shirt caused the first problem. I sat on the floor holding a sleeve in each hand, reeling backward as I noticed the stains around the collar. Every month or so, anxious about the gray strands multiplying around her temples, Mom would dye her hair a shade of brown carefully chosen from the dye kits at the drugstore. She wore the denim shirt for any kind of dirty job. She also wore the latex gloves that came in the kit, but the dye inevitably seeped through, and her hands would turn brown along with her hair. She'd tuck her chin while I spread the pasty dye on the back of her scalp. The chemical smell made us gag. Mom would squirm like a kid in church as I combed the dye through her hair and yelled at her to sit still. I clutched the shirt in my lap, remembering how those hair-dyeing sessions had always ended with the two of us laughing hysterically.

Clothing filled the trash bags easily enough, but the shoe bag was bulky. Mom's scuffed loafers fell atop her dirty white sneakers and the one pair of heels she owned but never wore. The last to go was the pair she wore most often: men's Sperry topsiders, the brown leather faded and worn. I tied the bag shut and tried not to deduce which shoes she must have worn to the pier.

The top of her dresser was cluttered with makeup and jewelry. I reached for her stained-glass jewelry box, wondering whether I should even open it, or just pack it up wholesale.

I lifted the lid. Its contents made about as much sense to me as had the past six weeks. The diamond ring my mother ate, slept, and showered in was lying on its side. She'd bought it for herself on the day her divorce became official and had been flaunting it on her ring finger ever since. It featured a huge swath of diamonds, a showy thing so unlike the rest of her demeanor. I had never known her to take it off. It seemed strange that I hadn't noticed this ring in all the times I'd scoured her apartment for clues while she was missing. Had I seen it then, it would have been just another bit of evidence I couldn't make sense of. *Indeterminable.* Along with her wallet and her coat, maybe she'd left her ring behind knowing that she wouldn't need any jewelry where she was going. Maybe she didn't want the water to ruin it. Or maybe she'd left the ring for me. I closed the box and walked out of the room.

I moved on to the kitchen. I opened the cupboard to find two porcelain bowls, fish painted along the rim. Mom and I had eaten our dinners out of these bowls every night the summer before. I would go running after work and come home sweaty, starving, and irritable. As I was peeling my damp clothes off one night in the living room—I'd never been modest about being naked in front of my mother—she called to me from the kitchen, my name over the dull thwack of her knife slicing vegetables.

"Linds, come here, I'll teach you this recipe you like," she said.

"I need to shower," I said, walking through the kitchen and closing the bathroom door as she looked expectantly at me. I had all the time in the world to learn her recipes, but right then I wanted to get cleaned up before dinner.

"You'll be sorry when I'm gone," she shouted as I turned on the faucet.

I yanked open the apartment door, stepped out onto the rusty fire escape, and tossed the dishes Frisbee-style. I leaned over the railing and watched the bowls shatter on the dirt driveway three flights below. Brad came rushing out.

"What the hell are you doing?" he said.

"I don't know," I mumbled, my body stooped over the railing.

"Don't be stupid. Go clean that up."

We didn't talk much the rest of the day. Trash bags filled our silence with a language all their own. Separate sounds for contents settling, tops being tied, and heavy loads being hefted down three flights of stairs to the trash out back. We were trudging through the unthinkable.

Chris, Brad, and I had packed up most of our mother's possessions by late afternoon. When it came time to haul everything to the dump, we lost our nerve, and the majority of the bags and boxes stayed on the apartment floor, packed up but not discarded. We drove the hour back to Dad's house as if we were three strangers on a bus.

Dad was standing at the sink with his back to us when we walked into the kitchen. He was always washing dirt or grease or paint off his hands, the remains of whatever project he'd just been working on. He had a rhythm to it, rubbing Gojo soap between his knuckles, up his forearms, and under his wide, flat fingernails. The soap came in a giant orange container Dad bought at Home Depot and kept stored under the sink. It was citrusy, gritty stuff. Dad had been tidying the yard all day, cutting the grass and moving his backhoe out of the driveway, preparing for Sunday's guests. I stood watching the soap swirl down the drain, waiting for him to say something. Waiting for him to say anything. I watched him dry his hands on a dishrag, just as slowly, before realizing that there was nothing he could say. *Unremarkable.* I felt his eyes pleading with me as I walked out of the kitchen.

I splashed cold water onto my face before crawling into bed. I curled up on my left side, holding my bad shoulder like a broken wing. I assumed my brothers and I had worked hard enough during the day to be rewarded with a full night's sleep, but grieving had nothing to do with what we did or didn't deserve.

We woke up Saturday overwhelmed and underslept, dreading all that had to be done before the service: calls to make, windows to wash, floors to vacuum, eulogies to write, and alcohol to buy. Michele made herself absent for the weekend, taking Maggie to a friend's house. It made sense to get her young daughter away from all the chaos and cleaning and cusswords and confusion that accompanied death.

My brothers and I also had to deal with our mother's *stuff.* The sooner we got those trash bags out of our sight and handed the apartment key back to her landlord, the better. I stayed behind to clean Dad's house while Chris and Brad rented a moving truck and loaded up the contents of Mom's apartment. I'd salvaged a few boxes, containing her photographs, jewelry, red suede purse, and other miscellaneous things that I wanted to sift through. These I hauled up to an empty room on the third floor of Dad's house. I didn't want her photos or jewelry to be sitting in a distant basement. My brothers crammed the U-Haul and left for the two-hour drive to the house in New Hampshire that our mother had bought a few weeks before disappearing.

By midafternoon, the first floor of my father's cavernous house had been scrubbed, dusted, and emptied of his tools that cluttered every available surface. Sawhorses, paint cans, power tools, and extension cords were often strewn about the foyer. Dad cleared out that room himself, because if anyone moved his tools, he said he'd never find them again. My brothers and I agreed that it'd be easier to call in a cleaning service, but Dad said scrubbing everything ourselves would be a good distraction—that and his belief that only lazy rich people hired others to clean their homes.

Aunts, uncles, cousins, and both my brothers' girlfriends had come over to help, but I was somehow separate in my chores, hearing them as if through layers of thick gauze. Death could do that, could take your ears and make them hear *off the end of a pier* when really someone was just asking if she could help you with the vacuuming.

The vacuuming took a while. The Oriental rugs in the dining and living rooms were covered in black and white dog hair. Tucker, Michele's mutt, loved to roll around on the rugs, and he shed all over the place. These two rooms had to be immaculate. They had the best views in the house and were where Sunday's guests would congregate. West Beach and the ocean were right out the windows. During awkward lapses in the remembering-my-mother conversations, people could always resort to talking about the view. West Beach, Misery Island, a storm-beaten dock, and a beach club: it was all there, right in my dad's front yard, my mom's New England.

The chores took me twice as long, since I had to do everything with my left arm, the sling keeping my right immobile. My whole body ached by the time I finished scrubbing the massive floor-to-ceiling window in the living room. The glass was streaky. I sat on the sill and looked out at the beach, Misery Island dark and jagged on the horizon. Craning my neck to the left, I thought I could almost see it. Just a few miles farther north, nestled in the crooked coastline of the Atlantic: Rockport Harbor, and a road ending in a pier, and a car submerged off the rocks, and a diver checking moorings, and what he found instead.

Ten years earlier, Dad had married his second wife in this same room.

My brothers returned around dinnertime. Chris and I went out to buy flowers and candles, leaving Brad to drive to the funeral home with Brodie, who'd been helping out since searching Millinocket almost a month earlier. A mile down the road from Dad's house, I wandered through Chapman's Greenhouse and stepped into a refrigerated room full of cut flowers. Blue and white hydrangeas: as soon as I saw them, I knew. Mom had turned our sprawling yard in North Andover into a giant garden, and I'd envisioned her doing the same at her new home in the mountains. Hydrangeas had flowered by our front door; she often cut a few blossoms to take to her mother at the nursing home. Because our grandmother was eighty-seven and her health was precarious, we didn't tell her what had happened, worrying that the news would be too much for her frail body. But the nurses called to say she'd been waking in the night shouting her daughter's name.

Hydrangeas were about all that felt *determinable* in such circumstances. I paid with Mom's credit card, signing her name in a weak imitation of her hand, every letter curving almost to the point of circularity.

Next we went to get some candles. We had discarded the waxy remains of at least ten in Mom's apartment the day before. I expected the candles to present themselves, just as the hydrangeas had. But we had to smell every one. We balanced them on various holders and debated whether to mix scents. We did everything short of lighting them in the store. Finally we agreed on White Linen—a clean scent, safe from sentimentality.

My brothers went to the liquor store while I headed out in search of a dress with Maglio, my best friend from high school, who'd driven back from college in western Massachusetts as soon as she'd heard the news. Dad couldn't believe that we wanted to serve alcohol on Sunday, but there was no way we'd survive the day without a buffer.

I couldn't bring myself to wear black. There was no room for darkness in my mother's wardrobe of untucked blouses, blue jeans, and dangling turquoise jewelry. We wandered through the brightly lit mall until I found a dress in Filene's Basement, where I'd shopped so many times with my mom. Maglio helped zip me in the dressing room and said it was the exact dress my mother would have picked out for me. So I charged that to her credit card too.

Meanwhile Dad went to BJ's Wholesale Club and bought two extra mattresses, wrestling them into the bed of his pickup truck. He also picked up a new washing machine, as the old one had broken since my brothers and I had arrived. He figured there might be some people looking for a place to sleep on Sunday night. Thought we might want clean clothes.

And then it was Sunday morning, the last day of April, the day of her memorial. Cassidy had arrived the night before. She was tying the satin ribbon on the waist of my dress when a car full of friends from school pulled into the driveway. I couldn't remember telling any of them what had happened and wondered how they knew. Cassidy went to entertain them while I finished getting ready. I'd hoped to slip into the kitchen for a glass of wine before seeing anyone. Brad glared up from the foyer as my heels clicked down the stairs a few minutes later.

"What are you wearing?" he muttered.

"What?"

"I can't believe you. Go change."

I pushed him aside, poured myself some red wine, and went back upstairs. I sat at my desk, picked up a pen, and opened my notebook. I told myself that whatever I wrote, I wouldn't reread until I gave the eulogy. I flipped through the last six weeks of illegible words and eyes sketched on every page, coming at last to a blank sheet. I took my best guess as to what a eulogy should entail, drained my glass, and went downstairs, leaving the sling on the bed.

And then it began, the greeting of old friends brought together by the worst kind of reunion. I said, "Thank you for coming," and they said, "You look beautiful." I said, "Thank you for coming," and they said, "God works in mysterious ways." I said, "Thank you for coming," and they said, "Your mother's in a better place now."

Everyone was there: Barbara Ann and her family, my uncle George and his girlfriend Linda, my aunt Patti and her husband, cousins who'd flown up from Florida, my mother's boss and colleagues, her old sailing buddies, my godparents, my fifth-grade teacher, my high school cross-country coach, my brothers' boyhood soccer teammates, my family, my friends, our past and present converging. Every time someone hugged me, my shoulder throbbed but I didn't mention it.

People kept telling me that I looked just like my mother. I didn't see the resemblance, and I didn't want to hear it. It felt like a lie meant to ease my passage through the day, to take some small part of my mother with me as I stumbled into the future. But all I felt was alone.

This was my first time meeting many of my mother's colleagues, although my brothers had been in contact with them throughout the search. They were as stunned as we were, and said they didn't know what they'd tell Cynthia, our mother's longtime student who'd been stripped of her main support system. They spoke of the "mystery garden" my mom had planted for one of their coworkers, how she'd mischievously refused to reveal what kinds of flowers were planted, saying only that she'd have to wait and see. But I didn't want to hear about my mom's good deeds or little surprises just then.

I had a feeling that most of the guests knew about the nature of my mother's death, though the obituary hadn't mentioned it and no one spoke of it at the service. Granite Pier seemed to hover behind every conversation I stepped into, an awful mirage that I couldn't be sure was even a reality. I couldn't be sure whether any of this was really happening. I walked around on autopilot.

Cassidy's parents were standing quietly by the window. They had driven five hours from their home in Vermont to be there. I made my way over to them and thanked them for coming. They had met my mom the previous winter, when they drove Cassidy down to visit over Christmas break. My mom had made lasagna, serving everyone helpings too big to finish.

"Oh, Linds," they said, hugging me between them.

A few hours later, I stood in the living room, facing the giant window I'd scrubbed from a stepladder the night before. I was in the middle of a circle of familiar faces, all but the one I most wanted to see. I opened my notebook, the turning of the pages suddenly the only sound in the room. About a hundred people were waiting for me to speak.

> One night last winter, my mom and I were driving to New Hampshire and I fell asleep like I always did, but this time she woke me up by putting all the windows down. I was freezing and she was laughing hysterically and I shouted over the rush of the wind, "You're crazy, Mom!" And she said, "I like being out there—it's less crowded."

I wanted to say it was a perfect drive, and I was lucky to have had such an incredible mother, but then I made the mistake of looking up from my notebook. It was like the eyes I'd been sketching for the past six weeks in my notebook had leaped off the page and were closing in on me from all sides. Some just stared, but most were crying, and I wondered if I'd said the wrong thing. My brothers had been smart in deciding not to make speeches.

Was this an example of God working in mysterious ways? Was the bottom of the Atlantic Ocean the "better place" I kept hearing about? The last thing I thought of—before the Oriental rug broke my fall—was who the hell did I think I was, wearing a white dress to my mother's memorial?

My friends picked me up off the floor. My dad kept his distance. My brothers ushered guests out to the porch. They thought I was drunk, and maybe I was. I hadn't eaten a thing all day, and had put my wineglass down only to read the eulogy.

We ran out of sandwiches and beer. I'd been in charge of making arrangements with the caterer and had underestimated how many people would show up. I hadn't counted on half the guests being men in their early twenties, my brothers' friends who had practically grown up at our house. I had forgotten how boys like that could eat, cleaning their plates whatever the circumstances.

After most of the guests had left, I went down to the beach with a few friends who were spending the night. We sat on the overturned hull of a dinghy and smoked pot. Cassidy abstained, but she blocked the wind and lit the bowl for me. The horizon disappeared in the dark and the stars jagged into the water. I got to that place—if only for a second—where the past forty days became a figment of my warped imagination. And then someone said she was freezing, and it was real again, and we went back to the house, my bare feet tracking sand all over the floor. Chris, Brad, Dad, and Michele were all standing in the kitchen. The room swayed as if I were standing on a dock. My friends went up to bed. The only fixed points were my brothers—both of them crying for the first time—and my dad, leaning against the refrigerator with his hands jammed in his pockets, his tie loosened, and his sleeves pushed up. I thought I saw him crying too, or maybe it was just that everything was reeling as I started to come down from my high.

"You've been smoking pot," Dad said.

"No I haven't."

"I can smell it."

"Okay, I have."

He kneaded his hands together. I'd let him down but I didn't care. All I wanted to know was when I could get my mom back and make all this go away. And if that weren't possible, then getting stoned and pretending I'd hallucinated this whole nightmare struck me as the least of our worries.

Chapter Six

THE DAY AFTER the service, I went back to Brown to finish out the last few weeks of the semester. I threw myself into paper writing and test taking, showing up for all my classes again. I completed whatever task was right in front of me because there was no other choice.

My mom's younger sister Patti had given me a dusty cardboard box at the memorial. Full of old jewelry, knickknacks, and mementoes she'd accrued over the years, it was better than all the sympathy cards I'd shoved in a drawer before leaving my dad's. If everyone had brought me a relic from my mother's life, maybe I could keep piecing clues together and figure out what had actually happened to her. I became obsessed with a sheet of Kodak negatives that I'd found in the box and taken back to school with me. Dated 1974, the negatives had remained perfectly preserved in a clear plastic sleeve for more than three decades.

Holding the negatives up to the light, I peered into a sliver of the past. What I saw was not the mother I knew but a younger, happier version of her, looking radiant in black and white, her arms around a charmingly handsome ghost of my father. After so many false leads and dead-end clues, the contact sheet offered something tangible, true, and baffling: a life that made no apparent sense in the context of how it had ended. So much was translucent when you held it up to the light.

I passed the last few weeks of the semester in the Rhode Island School of Design's darkroom, down the hill from Brown, where no one knew me and where I was free to make as many prints of these surreal images as I wanted.

Among pictures of my twenty-two-year-old parents sailing and windsurfing, there was a photograph of my mother, her face turned to something below the frame, hair pulled back in a bandanna, high cheekbones tanned and freckled as she stood in the cabin of the sailboat she and my father had just finished restoring. I wanted to know what she was looking at outside the frame. She could have been slicing a loaf of bread, preparing tuna sandwiches. She could have been plotting *Pippins*'s course on a nautical chart. Or she could've been looking *for* something—a bowline or a cold drink. Whatever her eyes were fixed on and whatever she was doing seemed important because I couldn't figure it out. I spent weeks making prints of this one photo, manipulating exposure and contrast, and even setting up a tripod and taking a similar photograph of myself, superimposing it digitally on top of the negative. I needed to see how we aligned. I inherited the map of her freckles, the shape of her earlobes (just visible below the edge of her bandanna), the curve of her nose, her dark brown hair turned wavy from a salt-licked breeze, her lust for the ocean, her love of my father, and her inability to understand what life would throw her way. Things outside the frame only to be guessed at: *What were you looking at, Mom? What were you looking for?*

I passed all my classes except for History of Modern Architecture, which I dropped. My shoulder healed and I threw the sling away. I packed up my room, hugged Cassidy good-bye, and hauled my bags down to the street corner.

Maglio and another high school friend picked me up. They tried to keep the mood light with pop on the radio and a stop at Taco Bell as we drove back to Massachusetts, but I felt like a zombie.

We arrived at my father's house a few hours later. Coming from my cramped dorm, my bedroom at Dad's felt big and foreign. The floors were a glossy oak and a fireplace stood adjacent to the bathroom. When Dad had begun renovations on the house fifteen years earlier, my room was the first one he tackled.

We had sponge-painted the walls light blue, and he surprised me with a desk he'd built, stenciling, "To Lindsay, I love you, Dad," inside the top drawer. I was seven and Dad had just moved out of a duplex in North Andover. The move was another transition that didn't make much sense to me, but I'd learned that asking questions often led to hearing bad things said by one parent about the other. Dad's new house became Mom's favorite example of how he had cheated her out of child support and spent it on a beachfront mansion instead.

But it was less like a mansion and more like a run-down hotel. Most of the rooms were empty, as if the guests had checked out in haste. One wing of the third floor was scattered with old clothes and a closet full of unused wedding gifts. Tiffany platters, silver frames, a picnic set, and dishes had been left behind by a teacher who'd lived up there.

I'd never thought of Dad's empty house as my home. It was good for hide-and-seek, and it had been good for the guests who stayed over the night of Mom's memorial, but it was not where I'd grown up. Mom's condemnation of the place left a bad taste in my mouth whenever I was there. I watched my friends unpack my bags. It was not my home, but it was the only place I had to come back to.

By the end of May, Chris and Brad had also moved into Dad's house. Three weeks had passed since the memorial, and we hadn't spoken much since then. We stood around the kitchen, unable to make eye contact. Brad sat at the counter going through a stack of Mom's unpaid bills, writing checks for her phone, electric, and credit cards. She'd apparently been neglecting all her bills for a few months. Mom had named Brad executor of her will, which didn't sit well with Chris, who assumed that as the oldest, he'd have the most authority. Mom's decision didn't surprise me, though. Brad had always been the one she consulted about money matters, taking his recommendations on cars to trade, investments to make, and properties to buy.

So Brad was in charge of cleaning up Mom's financial mess, which had recently come to include her new house. It was not a job I envied. He punched numbers on a calculator and rifled through bank statements while Chris, Dad, and I stood in the kitchen sipping tea. Dad asked about our summer plans.

Chris was moving from his apartment outside Boston into the third floor of Dad's house for a few months, to save on rent and buy an engagement ring for Elizabeth, his girlfriend of six years. Chris didn't have to say that he was also moving to be near Brad and Dad. Part of me wished I could be more like my brother, hopeful about the future even at a time when nothing made sense.

Brad had taken a summer job as caretaker of Misery Island, an eighty-six-acre hunk of land a half mile off the beach directly in front of Dad's house. His would be a summer without electricity, noise, and for the most part, people. He spread stacks of financial paperwork out on the dining room table so that he could row ashore and work on our mother's will whenever he wasn't maintaining the island's hiking trails.

I was bound for a camp in the woods of Maine, where I would teach photography in a log cabin beside a lake a few hours south of Millinocket. Once there, I hoped to be able to intuit whether my mom had gone to Maine before going out to sea. I yearned to know whether the snowmobiler, the nurse, and the policeman had been right, or if their sightings amounted to false hope, like so much else about the case. But mostly I needed to get away from my dad, my brothers, and the proximity of Rockport Harbor for a while.

Brad moved out to Misery the next day, and I promised to come see the island before I left. A few days later he motored ashore to pick me up in the Trustees of Reservations boat, a dented aluminum shell used for transporting lawn mowers to the island. I met him on the beach. Brad was always a more confident boater than I was; he knew just how close you could get to shore before the engine would run aground. He throttled into reverse as I waded out and climbed into the bow. Dad's house receded as we cut across the choppy water. I sat on a crate full of life jackets, my back to my brother and my mind tripping over all the things I wanted to say to him before we went our separate ways. The salty breeze tangled my hair and it felt so familiar to have a hull beneath me and a steady hand at the helm.

We coasted into the cove and waded ashore. The island had been named Misery by a shipbuilder marooned there for three days during a storm centuries earlier. Brad hauled the boat up the beach and looped the bowline around a boulder. I followed him across the rocky shore and up a steep grassy hill. A solar-paneled hut sat atop the ridge. Brad's accommodations consisted of a screened-in porch that led to a tiny room furnished with a mattress and little else. The screen was torn, the mesh peeling open to welcome mosquitoes and other winged creatures that would keep him up at night. Yellow flypaper hung in strips every few feet along the rafters. The yard had a view of the ocean from a hammock strung between two sturdy trees, where I knew my brother would sleep most nights.

"This is it," he said. "It's quiet at least."

This was my chance, the one I'd been waiting for. I wanted to know if Brad had been sleeping, eating, or spending time with friends over the past few weeks. I wanted to know whether he had reason to think our mom's death was his fault, as I thought it was mine.

He handed me a warm beer.

"So, how 'bout that tour?" I said.

We set off down the hill. Dad used to row us out to Misery for picnics, but we were young then, and everything looked different somehow. A resort and casino had been built on the island at the turn of the nineteenth century, but a few years shy of the Great Depression a brushfire swept across the fields and torched everything. Now the land was wild again, the stone foundations covered with moss and weeds. The Trustees of Reservations had bought the island to protect it. In the summertime, kids climbed atop the old foundations as if they were in a museum where they were finally allowed to touch things. Allowed to walk on stone skeletons.

Our mother's obituary had requested that guests make donations to the Trustees rather than bring flowers to her service. This had been Brad's idea. Flowers would all be dead within a week, he'd said, and what a waste that would be.

I walked a few paces behind my brother. We circled the grass-filled basin of an old saltwater swimming pool and headed toward the field in the middle of the island, passing the giant oak tree carved with initials and hearts. We trekked all the way around Misery. I was so busy thinking about what to say to Brad that barely a word passed between us. He had always been a silent observer, offering only the briefest of answers.

The sunset bled sloppily across the horizon. It was getting dark, time for me to go. We pushed the boat off the beach, climbed aboard, and floated out under a faint moon. Brad started the engine and we made our way out of the cove, weaving between mooring balls that shone like giant eggs in the pitching water.

"How did all this happen?" I said.

"Don't ask me."

I watched the prow of the boat as it sliced open the water. We reached the shore a few minutes later. Up past the beach grass Dad's house was dark and empty looking.

Brad hadn't timed the reversal very well, and I had to hop out and push hard on the hull to keep the boat from running aground. It was deeper than I expected and the frigid water came up to my waist. Brad busied himself with the engine while I gave the bow a final shove.

"Have a good summer," he said.

"You too."

I walked up the beach, through the wooden door cut into the stone wall, and up the granite steps to the house. I turned back to the ocean and watched my brother grow smaller and smaller until I could no longer separate his boat from the endless expanse of water.

Dad drove me to Maine the next morning. We didn't talk much on the ride, but silence didn't surprise me anymore. We passed through at least three tollbooths, slowing to roll down the windows and dig up quarters. I was glad that Dad didn't have an E-Z Pass. I'm sure he could have gotten one for free, as the company he'd spent twenty years working for—moving from engineer up to president and CEO—invented similar transponders before E-Z Pass won the major New England turnpikes. Tolls, everywhere I looked.

We got off the interstate near Augusta, and once we passed the Wal-Mart Supercenter, signs of life grew sparse.

"You sure about this?" Dad said.

I didn't know whether he was asking about the directions, my summer plans, or both. He thought it risky that I was going so far away so soon, but I wanted none of his suggestions on what would be good for me. His presence heightened her absence, and I resented him for calling his house my home.

I traced my finger on the map and guided us down single-lane roads riddled with potholes and flanked by farmland. We passed countless grazing cows, but not a single person. *God's country:* that's what I knew my mom would call such a road. Not so much because she was a devout believer but more because it was just one of those phrases she repeated. They were always on my mind now: *Re-al-it-y check!* whenever I was being grandiose. *Batten down the hatches!* when the rain suddenly sluiced into the cabin of our sailboat.

Dad didn't factor into any of these memories, though. I kept my eyes on the map and told him where to turn. We pulled into the camp after five hours on the road.

"It looks like a country club," Dad said.

He was right. I had never been to sleepaway camp as a child. A horse stable, rock-climbing wall, and clusters of deluxe log cabins were not exactly what I'd pictured. A grounds crew was hard at work, mulching and manicuring every inch of the sprawling property.

Meeting with the camp director, I learned that I wouldn't be living with any campers, as I was not a regular counselor but head of the photography department—a last-minute promotion that meant I'd be managing a staff in addition to teaching. The director knew I had recently lost my mother, but I hadn't told her all the specifics. I didn't want her opinion of me to be based on what I'd just been through. The regular counselors would arrive in a few days, and for the time being, I had a whole cabin to myself. Dad and I lingered on our tour of the facilities. All of a sudden, I could not bear the thought of him leaving. But the drive was long and he needed to get back on the road. I said I'd be fine and hugged him with my eyes clamped tight.

A few days later, an exhausting round of orientation activities and safety drills commenced. I sat on the soccer field surrounded by throngs of counselors, most of whom I'd avoided so far. The director shouted over a microphone.

"Should one of your campers go missing during a swimming session, immediately grab the other counselors and lifeguards to form a human chain. Link arms and spread your legs shoulder-width apart, making sweeping motions under the water. Your feet would—God forbid—bump into the submerged body."

The camp director was about five feet tall; her voice was the biggest thing about her, booming and reverberating. I plucked at the grass and waited for it to be over. Like all the tests I would face in my mother's absence, no one else knew it was a test—no one here knew that she'd sunk too deep for the missing bather method—and I could only hope to pass it by acting tough even when I wasn't. People kept talking about my mom dying, even when they had no idea.

Despite such moments, camp life provided the distraction I needed. It was a relief to look like everyone else, wearing staff T-shirts with moose silhouetted on our backs. I befriended a few other counselors and we schemed about camping trips on our days off. Most were from the Midwest or farther west, and I was relieved that they had likely not read about the story in the *Boston Globe,* or seen my brothers on the local news.

There was one person I confided in, though. Sitting in the cafeteria the first week of orientation, I whispered the whole story to Torin, a counselor I'd just met. He stared at me with his brown saucer eyes and offered me one of his chicken fingers. It seemed as good a response as any. I dipped the offering in his pool of ketchup and from then on we spent all our free time together.

One night while we were sitting on the dock he handed me a picture he'd drawn. My mother, abstracted into a whole marker box of colors and contours, rising out of the water, toes pointed and hands arcing up to the sky. When I was around Torin, I could almost believe that my mom's death was reversible, that a drawing could save her from Rockport Harbor and send her flying.

I spent my days teaching photography. Sitting on a picnic table while twenty campers crowded around, I dismantled old Nikons and demonstrated the tiny mirror inside, showing them how the camera flips the image onto the filmstrip. They fidgeted and whispered, too young to care about the inverted relationship between aperture and shutter speed. They wanted to run around the campgrounds and take photos of their friends. The light meters in the old cameras were mostly broken anyway, and after a few lessons I set them loose with a roll of film and a camera for every two campers, shouting instructions to take action shots, portraits, and textures.

Nights I walked down the gravel hill and let myself into the darkroom to develop the campers' film. Since high school I had known perfect solitude in opening film canisters in the dark, prying their tops off with can openers. I guided roll after roll onto plastic spools, feeling the edges catch and glide, securing them in lightproof containers before flipping on the lights and flooding the containers with acrid chemicals. I loved the ritual nature of photography, the combination of mindlessness and precision that the darkroom required. It let my mind wander only in measured intervals, until the film needed to be unwound and clothespinned up to dry.

Most of the campers didn't have the attention span the darkroom required. I ended up developing all the film and most of their prints myself, and few of them remembered my name, but I didn't mind. It was enough to watch their images appear in the developer: snapshots of kids by the lake, their small hands raised in peace signs.

I'd made it through two months of camp and had one more to go. Late in July I decided that my body had grown accustomed to Prozac, the antidepressant that I'd been taking for almost two years. The pills had given me little solace during the six-week search, and I wanted them out of my system. Consulting a doctor about going off the medication didn't occur to me; the school psychiatrist had written me a hasty prescription and told me to keep in touch, but I was not good at such things. I flushed the blue-and-white capsules down the toilet one morning while my bunkmates snored in their sleeping bags.

Within a few days I was regretting my assumed authority over my brain's chemical imbalances. My hands were vibrating at high frequencies. Calling my family was the last thing I wanted to do; it would be kinder to let them assume I was fine. Better to ignore the withdrawal symptoms and turn my attention back to the darkroom. But it suddenly seemed impossible to teach fifty kids a day about developer, stop, and fixer, about test strips and toner. I was starting to remember March. And against my will, there was April, as stark and focused as a glossy print, drip-drying from a clothespin.

I woke one morning later that week with the heat cloying and the air stagnant around my top bunk. My mother's Subaru rattled off the pier as I rubbed the sandmen out of my eyes. The image seemed sharper somehow, as if the dull shroud of distraction had been lifted, and the camp counselor charade could not sustain me any longer.

I rolled over and saw the book I'd been trying to read resting on the window ledge: Joan Didion's *Year of Magical Thinking*. I'd been unable to concentrate every time I picked it up, although one passage had been on my mind for weeks—first because the sentiment seemed bizarre, and then because I realized how familiar two lines about cleaning out her late husband's closet felt:

I could not give away the rest of his shoes. I stood there for a moment, then realized why: he would need shoes if he was to return.

I'd trashed my mom's topsiders not three months before, watching them fall into the folds of yet another black bag. But instead of hoping for her to return—after six weeks of wanting nothing else, this I couldn't long for anymore—I'd been guessing at what shoes she must have worn when she died.

I climbed down from my bunk and put on my staff T-shirt, shorts, and flip-flops. I walked to the darkroom, realizing, as if for the first time, that there was no undoing what my mother had done. Drowning was for keeps. She was not coming back, no matter how much I repented, begged, drank, or denied it. But maybe I could go to her.

I worked in the darkroom all day helping campers develop their prints. We crowded around the chemical baths, submerging paper and agitating the developer until the dark tones surfaced. It amazed me every time that an image would appear only when submerged and only under the dim red glow of a safelight.

The campers kept whining about how much faster digital photography was. There was no convincing such an instant-gratification crowd about the value of the process. I tired of hearing them complain and sent them out to the porch to wait until the bell signaled their next activity. I stood in the darkroom, rinsing prints long after their chemical traces washed away.

There was a free period at the end of the camp day when I was supposed to keep the darkroom open. The campers always chose waterskiing or rock climbing over photography, so I didn't think twice about locking up early. I was dizzy from inhaling chemicals all day. I walked to my cabin and put my bathing suit on under my shorts and T-shirt. I went to the bathroom and grabbed a plastic Gillette razor out of the shower. I pocketed it, took a few of my bunkmate's Band-Aids, and bounded down the steps in the direction of the staff dock.

I had the secluded area to myself, as the other counselors were busy trying to corral their campers to dinner. I climbed onto the huge boulder beside the dock. I took the razor out of my pocket and placed it in a stony crevice. I peeled off my T-shirt and stepped out of my shorts.

All I had to do was dive.

All I had to do was swim out to where I could no longer touch the bottom and then tread until my limbs grew tired. Let my legs dangle, let my freckled arms rest. Let the water still. Watch the sun set. Allow the water to entice me under. This was not dying. It was a way to live again, because living had always meant being with my mom.

The razor was more of an afterthought, a bright idea I'd had while changing into my bathing suit. I would let a little of the poison out of my wrists, and then slap on a few Band-Aids before any real harm was done. The sadness would trickle out and I would doctor the wounds. Or I could just swim out to meet her, spilling a thin red line underwater. By then it wouldn't matter.

But when I held the razor to my wrist, I couldn't drag it across, not deep enough to do any real damage anyway. The twin metal blades were almost rusting. I tried to sharpen them on the rock, but what I really needed was a straight razor. I considered going back to the darkroom for an X-Acto knife, but all of a sudden I felt so tired, as if I'd been sitting on this rock for centuries. Swimming suddenly seemed much too difficult.

I was hugging my knees to my chest when I heard someone leap onto the rock behind me. Without turning around, I knew it was Torin. He always met me on the rock before dinner.

I didn't say anything. I kept my eyes locked on the water. He saw the razor then. He grabbed my arms and pried them loose from my knees, flipping my wrists palms up to the waning light.

"Linds, what are you doing?"

I looked up from his hands, still gripping my wrists, but looser, like bracelets. He was unsmiling for once, and his Midwestern manners were unable to mask his horror. I swayed back and forth, saying, "I'm sorry," rhythmically, my mantra.

I'm sorry for your loss—wasn't that what everyone had said at the memorial?

But it didn't matter what I said. The razor and the Band-Aids were signaling their own alarm. Torin took the razor, jumped off the rock, and ran off through the woods.

He was gone for only a few minutes, but in that time, I saw how badly I'd messed up. A whirl of bats came swooping overhead, alighting over the lake as they did every night at dusk. I had promised myself that I would never do what my mother had done, no matter how fractured I felt. But it had seemed so simple, swimming until I couldn't tread anymore.

My brooding was interrupted by the sounds of two people approaching, twigs snapping underfoot. The camp director climbed onto the rock while Torin hung back, shredding the bark off a stick. He wouldn't look at me.

The director crouched down next to me. "Torin's really worried about you," she said.

"I'm sorry."

She suggested we go for a walk, and I knew I didn't have much choice in the matter. Torin lingered behind as we walked up the path. I wanted to punch him; I wanted him to hold me. There was too much to work out in so short a distance. The director's golf cart was parked on the gravel path. I realized that Torin would not be coming. I was in big trouble, the kind you have to face alone.

I closed my eyes as we sped up the hill toward the office. The director led me into a small room with two plastic chairs and several photographs of smiling campers on the wall. One moment she was speaking into her walkie-talkie, and the next, the room was full of people. Various managers and directors crowded around me as I studied my hands, clasped prayer-style in my lap, although I was not praying. It seemed pointless to tell everyone that I only wanted to go swimming. Nothing in my head seemed to make sense once I said it out loud. *Sorry* meant a million other things. I was too exhausted to defend myself.

The shuffling of papers sounded unnecessarily loud and harsh as the director searched for my emergency contact information. This was the first time I had listed anyone other than my mom as the person to call if something happened to me. If only I could tell this room full of strangers that I'd been too chicken to draw my own blood. I hadn't really wanted a sharper razor. But the director was already dialing my father's number.

"Let me talk to him. I can explain," I said.

It was no use. She wouldn't give me the phone. She said hello to my father and went on to tell him that I'd been sitting on a rock with a razor by my side. It was difficult to breathe upon hearing such a thing and picturing my father's fallen face.

"Let me talk to him."

But nobody was listening to me.

Before I had time to process what was happening, I was guided into the backseat of a minivan and driven away from camp. The director kept glancing at me in the rearview mirror. I tried to look as docile as possible, clasping my hands as if continuing an earlier prayer. My fingers were trembling and I tried to still them by pressing hard knuckle to knuckle.

We took the road past Wal-Mart and got on the interstate heading south, taking the exit for the hospital forty-five minutes later. I was too tired to care where we were going. At least I no longer had to pretend that I was fine.

In the waiting room, a middle-aged man calmly filled out paperwork as a gash on his head bled down his neck and stained his wifebeater. I tried not to stare. The director handed me a *People* magazine. I flipped the pages until a nurse called my name and took me down a beige hallway. The door sealed shut and the confusion of the waiting room hushed into metallic silence. I followed the nurse through a maze of hallways, ending in a small, stark room with a bed and a curtain for a door.

The nurse handed me a paper gown in exchange for every article of my clothing, as well as my cell phone. She stuffed all of it into a plastic bag. I pulled the gown tighter around me, but it was cold on the metal table without my underwear.

Goose bumps on my bare legs. A name tag bracelet on my wrist. A doctor hurrying down the hallway. I wanted to be anywhere other than alone in the ER. I didn't understand how coping had led to a paper gown.

A nurse finally brought me a hospital phone. I called Dad's house and Brad answered. Apparently the news had already reached Misery, and Brad had come ashore.

"You can't do what she did, Lindsay," he said.

"I'm sorry—"

"How do you think I felt getting that call again? You can't do that to me."

I pictured him cutting the engine, tipping the motor up, and jumping off the bow.

"I'm sorry."

Sprinting up the beach, under the stone archway, and up the three flights of granite stairs to the house.

"Promise me. Promise me right now that you'll never do what she did, no matter how bad it hurts."

And I *was* sorry, sorry to make him run his breath ragged at my expense. Sorry that I'd induced the same fear in his voice as on the day Mom had failed to show up for work. Sorry that I was sitting in an emergency room.

"Okay."

"Promise me."

"I promise."

"Dad's on his way."

I handed the phone back to the nurse in exchange for a Styrofoam cup of warm ginger ale. I never wanted to come that close to being my mother again. I drained the soda and sank my teeth into the Styrofoam, gnawing around the edge until the nurse held out her hand. I gave her the cup and watched her deposit it in the trash with a quick pump of her shoe on the can's silver pedal.

Night came but I couldn't tell inside the emergency room, where it was lit up around the clock. I sat in bed with a thin blanket pulled up around my gown. I knew it was late when my dad came rushing in, because the hospital was at least four hours from Massachusetts, and everything had gone wrong around dinnertime.

"I'm her father, I'm her father," I heard him saying.

I sat up in bed as he pushed aside the curtain. I had never seen my dad cry before. He'd been stone-faced at my mom's memorial. The tears were much worse. He hugged me, tentatively at first, and then seeing that I wasn't as fragile as the phone call had led him to believe, harder, and harder, until my face was pressed up against his wet cheek. His hands were rough and warm on my back where the gown slit open. All I could say was "sorry," but Dad didn't expect me to say anything. He understood.

Michele had come too. Her blond hair was cut short, her blue eyes searing me from her angular face. She had always been thin, but as I sat on the edge of the bed while she hugged me for maybe the fifth time in my life, her muscles felt as if they'd been chiseled away under her cotton T-shirt. She had never met my mom. And although they shared the same first name, they could not have been more different. "You have to open up to us, Lindsay," she said.

It was all too bright in the hospital's fluorescents.

I closed my eyes and let Dad deal with the doctor and the paperwork. The hospital released me late in the night. I curled up on the cramped backseat of Dad's truck and fell asleep to the thrumming of the diesel engine. I woke to daylight in his driveway. The camp director packed up my bunk and shipped my stuff to Massachusetts. Two cardboard boxes arrived on the porch a few days later, red-ink stamped HEAVY all around my father's address. *Heavy* was the nicest way she could think to fire me.

Seeing my brothers was the worst part of it. I could refer to the whole thing only as the Swimming Incident, a title I much preferred to "suicide attempt." But to those on the other end of the phone line, how else could a razor translate? Chris stole sideways glances at my wrists when I returned, confused and relieved to see my skin and veins intact. Brad had returned to Misery and I didn't see him that first day back. I figured Dad had already called him to report that I was okay. I slept through the afternoon and woke for dinner.

That night, Chris did his best to distract me by talking about his wedding plans. He had bought a ring and Elizabeth had said yes. They were house hunting in New Hampshire. They had been dating since their sophomore year at the University of New Hampshire, and our mother had always expected them to get married. I tried to be excited for them, or at least to smile no matter how I felt, as Mom had done so well.

The next morning, I sat on the porch trying to write a letter to Torin. I looked out at the bay and saw Brad slicing across the water in the Trustees boat, the sun glinting off the metal hull. I shoved the letter into my pocket as Brad glided ashore (I'd gotten as far as "Dear Tor, I didn't mean to—"). He dragged the boat a ways onto the sand. He walked up the beach and disappeared momentarily as he passed through the beach grass and the heavy wooden door leading up to the yard. He climbed the stone steps and walked barefoot across the lawn, finally dropping into the deck chair beside me.

"What happened to you?" I said.

Brad was wearing only a bathing suit. His ribs stuck out like a ladder on his tanned body and his shoulder blades threatened to slice through his taut skin. His cheekbones were hollow, his nose sunburned and peeling. He had lost about thirty pounds from his already lean six-two frame, and all this in the two months since I'd last seen him, when mono and our mother had stolen his appetite.

His shaggy black hair was salted with an alarming number of white strands, making him look eerily like Dad, whose hair had grayed slowly, beginning the stately progression to white over the past few years. Dad was fifty-four years old, though, and Brad was twenty-one. He was going gray over the course of a summer.

"Nice to see you too."

I knew we wouldn't talk about the Swimming Incident. Certain things could be said only over the phone, certain promises made only across great distances. Sitting on the porch at our father's house, squinting at a beach opening bright with umbrellas, we could only be how we had always been: brother and sister, preferring silence to small talk. And when the silence began to weigh on me, I went inside to make him a sandwich.

I spent most of August walking on the beach, building sand castles with Maggie and jumping into the waves. I knew I wouldn't swim too deep. The razor felt like a mistake whose consequences I'd fortunately escaped. I couldn't help but wonder whether my mother's demise had followed a similar thought process. Sitting in her car on Granite Pier, had stepping on the gas pedal somehow seemed an easy thing to do? Had hitting the water meant something other than dying?

But what I'd done seemed as much a consequence of going off my medication as anything else. Flushing my Prozac down the toilet was a delayed reaction to a conversation I'd had with my mom about a year earlier. She'd come to Providence to visit. We were out to dinner at a Thai restaurant, a bring-your-own-beer place, a bottle of wine between us. I was underage but the waiter didn't care and neither did my mom. I'd just told her how much better I was feeling about college thanks to therapy and medication.

"What—I'm not good enough for you? You have to tell your problems to a stranger?" she hissed.

She pushed pad Thai around on her plate, twisting the noodles maniacally.

"Of course you're good enough."

"And what problems could you possibly have? Haven't I given you everything you've ever wanted?"

"I'm sorry."

She finished the wine and called for the check. My eyes were watering and my nose running, but Mom didn't so much as look at me as we left the restaurant. We drove back to my dorm in silence. She turned to face me as I reached for the door handle.

"Not everyone pops pills to solve their problems," she said.

I willed myself not to cry as I got out of the car. Occasional comments like this were usually softened by my mother's unwavering affection for me, but this was a level of harshness I'd never heard before. Every antidepressant I'd swallowed since then had tasted of weakness and condemnation. And so I flushed them and told myself to be stronger, all the while thinking that not everyone drives off a pier to solve her problems. But if my mother had somehow survived that cataclysmic crash, I would not have said such a thing to her. I would have bitten my tongue and tried to understand.

Chapter Seven

DAD HAD SUDDENLY become my decision-making parent. He wanted me to return to school in September, but I refused to go back to a campus that felt more like a crime scene. Chris and Brad took Dad's side, arguing that classes would give me some structure, or at least distraction. It would be my junior year, which meant two more years of walking past those four barrels in the quad that had stood sentinel as Brad called to tell me that our mom hadn't shown up for work. Trash, Paper, Bottles, Mixed Containers. I called the dean and asked about taking a semester off. She suggested I take at least a year. I didn't know what I'd do instead of school, but anything seemed better, and I applied for part-time work around Beverly.

I also bought a fifteen-year-old Jeep Cherokee I'd found on Craigslist. I knew my mom would never have let me drive a rust bucket with no air bags, but air bags hadn't saved her. Dad was as good a mechanic as any and said the Jeep was a steal for fifteen hundred bucks.

He spent the better part of August fixing the brakes, shocks, U joints, and muffler so I'd have a shot at passing state inspection. Shimmying out from under the car with grease on his hands and dirt in his hair, he'd moan that ninety percent of the job was getting the screws loose from under all the layers of rust.

In the heat of the day I'd bring him iced tea and hang around to hand him tools. He claimed it was simple logic, like a puzzle, the way the parts fit together to make an engine. Said anyone could be a mechanic if he had the patience to figure it out. I was just glad he was saving me the expense of hiring one. By dinnertime his hands would be covered in grease, but he didn't mind.

His parental love took an entirely different form from what I was used to. Mom would have bought me a newer car or paid for a mechanic. But Dad took the same approach he had his whole life: if something was broken, he would fix it. And if he didn't know how, he would learn. It seemed his divorce had been the one thing he couldn't fix, or even patch into something amicable for the sake of his kids. But although he was fixing my car, I couldn't make eye contact when he told me, almost pleadingly, that he loved me. He would do anything for me, that much I knew. But he couldn't bring my mom back.

He couldn't say the right thing, either. If he talked about the weather or what was for dinner, he was insensitive. If he offered to help Brad untangle the specifics of our mom's will, he was plotting a way to take a dead woman's money. I never stopped to consider what it must have felt like to lose the mother of your three children, a woman you'd shared a bed with for almost two decades.

One day I was making a sandwich; food had lost its taste but still I ate. Dad was mixing lemonade from the industrial-sized tub of bright yellow powder that he bought at B.J.'s. All his food came in quantities that would last through the season. I still wanted an answer to the question I'd asked Brad on the boat ride back from Misery a few months earlier.

"How did this even happen?" I said.

"Just look at how your mother lived her life."

I stormed out of the house and walked down to the end of the beach, where the smokestacks of Salem loomed on the horizon and a jagged pile of rocks made for a good brooding spot. I wanted spoon-fed sympathy, not this hammer-and-nails kind of love that Dad was offering.

He'd always been able to convey a whole argument in a single statement. I knew, as soon as he asked me to look at how my mom had lived her life, that her car ending up on the bottom of Rockport Harbor had probably not been accidental, as I still wanted to believe. I stood on the beach hurling rocks into the water.

Pressurized debris: that was what Dad was asking me to consider.

Seaweed choked the shoreline and squished under my toes as I walked back to the house. I rinsed my feet under the garden hose and cut across the lawn, passing the workshop where Dad was building something or other. I knew he wouldn't apologize and so we avoided each other for a day or two.

Later that week Dad and I got in his truck and drove to Salem for an appointment we'd both been dreading. Upon releasing me from the hospital in Maine a month earlier, the doctor had extracted a promise from my father that we would seek counseling together. Dad could talk for hours about building doors or dressers, about hanging drywall or laying shingles, but feelings were not a topic of conversation that we often dared to broach. I had my doubts about how a therapist could help, but a deal was a deal.

In the therapist's office we sat on separate couches. Dad kept wringing his hands and glancing out the window, his blue eyes unreadable under his thick brows. He fumbled for answers to the therapist's questions, but it wouldn't have mattered what he said. Even if he had begged my forgiveness, taken blame for my mother's death, and poured me a nice tall glass of vodka, I still would have found a way to condemn him.

I knew, as soon as we left the office and silently got back in the truck, that staying at his house for the fall would be even harder than returning to school. I called the dean back and asked her to enroll me again. The fall semester started in a week.

There was one last task to be done before leaving. My brothers had been giving me a hard time for not helping with all the postdeath paperwork. There were bills to pay, accounts to close, and insurance companies to deal with. Wanting to prove my usefulness, I got in my Jeep one morning and drove to Mom's new house in New Hampshire. The least I could do was throw things away.

Chris had informed me that the basement contained twenty or so boxes that he and Brad had transported from Mom's apartment in Newburyport, and twice as many from our childhood home in North Andover. I'd donate what I could to Goodwill and chuck the rest.

We had put the house on the market right away. I suspected

that Mom would have wanted us to keep the place, bring our own children there in the future and tell them stories about their grandmother: how she could turn a pile of rocks into a thriving garden or sail through a squall that would make most sailors seek harbor. But our lives were elsewhere. Neither my brothers nor I could live there in the foreseeable future, and maintaining the house was costing us. The thought of owning an empty vacation home in our early twenties was absurd; the thought of having my own children someday was terrifying. I didn't want to make the same mistakes she had. Mom had loved my brothers and me to the point that we became her whole world. I couldn't imagine a mother's love taking any other form.

It shouldn't have been so draining to sell a house without memories, but the potential of my mother's new life made it feel like more than just a vacant house. She had come so close to starting over. Her new house wasn't near the ocean, but the mountains were her second love. Paid in cash, no mortgage, no looking back. The moving truck receipt I'd found early in the search fueled my slow-burning hope that things were still going according to plan. Even after my mom's body had been found, I took comfort in that receipt. It allowed me to believe that what had happened on Granite Pier wasn't premeditated but was rather a moment of despair on a dark night, a plan to start over stalled out and sunk. Had driving into the water been a horrible split-second decision whose consequences she hadn't paused to consider?

I'd discussed the possibilities with my brothers somewhere in the fog that followed April. Brad said he suspected our mom was bipolar and had probably suffered a depressive episode that led her to Granite Pier. Chris responded by saying that what had happened had been a long time coming. I said nothing. Telling ourselves that she could have been bipolar was the same as telling ourselves that she was in a fugue during the forty days she was missing: comforting at times, but ultimately useless. Calling her crazy wasn't going to bring her back or make her absence any less acute. We just wanted to know what had caused her to leave in the first place. We agreed that she had likely needed mental health care of some kind. But therapy, according to our mother, was a crutch for self-indulgent weaklings.

But as I drove the two hours to my mother's vacant house, I wasn't thinking about what had made her drive off a pier. I was wondering whether I'd always feel so alone. I had told myself that I needed to become completely self-sufficient: I shouldn't burden my friends and I shouldn't ask too much of my family. Maglio had practically insisted that she help me sort through my mother's things, but I'd told her that I needed to do it alone. The moment I pulled into the deserted driveway I realized what a fool I was. No one would ever stand in for my mother, but self-imposed isolation wasn't going to solve anything, either.

The sun glinted off the green tin roof of the cookie-cutter house. I was sure I could blow it over if I puffed hard enough. The mountains looked made of cardboard. Stage props for a life my mother couldn't bear to live.

I gripped the steering wheel, doubting that I could really go through with the task or even enter the house by myself. Just seeing the place filled me with dread. Had anyone bothered to throw out the notes we left for her while she was missing, or would they still be sitting on the kitchen counter, collecting dust? *Dear Mom, we really want to talk to you.*

I backed out of the driveway. A mile down the road I found a convenience store and parked, leaving my keys in the ignition. I grabbed a six-pack of Bud Light, a bag of chips, and a roll of heavy-duty trash bags, walking to the register trying to look as casual as possible. It was not yet noon and I was not yet twenty-one. The cashier didn't card me, and as I drove back to the house, it seemed an act of grace to have a six-pack on my lap, to have alcohol to ease me through.

I found the key and walked into the house. I stood in the kitchen and ran my hand along the cold burners of the cookstove. There were no notes to my mother on the counter.

The mountains squatted like giants beyond the floor-to-ceiling sliding glass doors. But I wasn't here to admire the view. I carried my supplies down to the basement. The boxes were stacked three deep wall to wall, evil cardboard creatures that would no doubt spawn exponentially the moment I made any progress.

I cracked open my first beer as I came across the picture box: hundreds of loose photographs stored in an old wicker basket, having accumulated for years in my mom's bedroom closet. I sat down on the cool concrete floor and dug in.

Hours later, I'd gotten no further than making a circle of photos on the floor, in the middle of which I sat, Indian-style, weeping. Most of the pictures documented summers aboard our sailboat, *Pippins:* diving off the boom, jumping from the pulpit, and rowing our dinghy, *Chuckles,* which we roped to the stern whenever we set sail. Happiness, in the simplest form I'd ever known it, existed along the swell of the Atlantic. Mom and her crew: Chris, Brad, and Lindsay. Swimming in that frigid New England water left our shoulders golden and our fingers pruned. Ropy sailors' bracelets preserved a strip of white skin around our ankles, evidence of how much the sun had darkened us by August. We would always be here, together on the water, just waiting for the next summer. Another round of birthdays, lost teeth, new bathing suits, and a few more inches. And Mom, there to catch it all on film.

Before I knew it, I was drunk and the afternoon was gone. I was sitting in the dark.

I returned the photos to the wicker basket, sliding it into an alcove under the basement stairs. Gathering my beer cans, I ran up the stairs and through the shadowy house. I locked the door and hurried out to my car without looking back. I hadn't meant to drink so much. I drove extra carefully to compensate.

Going through North Conway I passed the Muddy Moose and Horsefeathers, restaurants my mom had taken me to on countless occasions. I got back on Route 16, which I'd follow south to Massachusetts before making my way east, to the ocean, to my father's house. Outside of town, the one-lane highway was dark and mostly empty.

I knew I'd have to call my brothers and tell them I hadn't gotten very far with the housecleaning. They'd given me a test and I had failed. I'd become the useless one, the daughter paralyzed by sadness. That grieving required *feeling* so much seemed burden enough—that it demanded so much *doing* seemed wholly unfair.

I started looking for barren stretches of road where I could get rid of the beer cans. I didn't want the evidence in my car, but I didn't want to stop until I was far away from this state where you had to live free or die. New Hampshire's Old Man of the Mountain had recently crumbled into a valley far below, the rocky profile of his nose and jaw worn down after decades of watching over northbound travelers. Finally falling, he too had died. Tall pines loomed off the shoulder of the road. I rolled down my window and tossed the cans one after another, somewhere south of where the old man used to keep a lookout.

Two days later, I packed up my things and left for school, refusing my father's offer to help and instead cramming everything into the car myself. The only room that the housing office had left was a tiny single in the religious dorm. I carried my bags to my new room, stepping over a group of students huddled in the hallway, which I assumed was some kind of Bible study. The pious students were on my left, while a sorority loomed adjacent to my room on the right. This had to be some kind of cosmic joke. Bible thumpers in the hallway and high-heeled sorority sisters clomping up and down the stairs late at night. I doubted I'd make a single friend all year. Cassidy was taking a semester abroad in South Africa. I was on my own.

September crawled past. I rarely answered my phone when Dad called, day after day. Chris and Brad had the annoying habit of calling multiple times in a row instead of leaving messages. Whenever I saw four missed calls from Chris, I braced myself to hear that Brad had died in a horrible car crash, or vice versa. In these mangled visions, it would always turn out that the accident was too related to March to really be accidental. When I answered the phone, it was to make sure everyone was okay, then to tell my family to leave me alone or at least leave a message.

I was going through the daily motions that college required, but as the fall dragged on, I retreated further and further into the past. I'd taken a photo album back to school, one I'd found in my mom's dresser as we ransacked her apartment. She was always snapping photos, documenting every soccer game, sailing trip, and holiday gathering with our names and ages scrawled on the backs. But she never made albums. Pictures eventually moved from the overstuffed kitchen drawer to the wicker basket in her closet, losing their attendant envelopes and negatives, becoming the picture puzzle that would sidetrack me on the basement floor for hours.

But this album was different. The windows were cut square for Polaroids, a format I'd never seen in my lifetime. The photographs showed two people I almost recognized. There were my parents, in their early twenties, the same age I had just reached. These snapshots told the story not of where my mother had gone but of the strangely happy place from which she had come.

My parents first met at Bliss Marine, a boating-supply store where they were both working the summer between their freshman and sophomore years of college. I imagined them flirting by the register, going out for milk shakes after their shift. They had both grown up in Massachusetts. Dad had gone to an all-boys high school and was studying engineering at Princeton, which in the early '70s was practically an all-male field. My mom was the first pretty girl he met.

They continued to date all through college. My mom would drive from her childhood home in Wellesley to Princeton in her VW Bug on weekends. They graduated in 1974 and were married a year later. They were twenty-two years old. My dad got a job as an engineer at Gillette, while my mom worked as a dentist's assistant and a waitress.

Their honeymoon phase consisted of fixing up a thirty-foot wooden sailboat that they bought. My mom had grown up sailing with her family, and Dad had always been a handyman, so buying a fixer-upper of a boat seemed logical enough.

Dad said that my mom thought of *Pippins,* and though I'd always loved the name painted on the stern of our old boat, I never asked her how she'd chosen it. It seemed a given, which was the same way I had always seen my mother—having no life before my brothers and me, and no foreseeable end to the one we'd made together. But I was wrong. Here was this whole life she had lived before us.

In the first photo, my parents are wearing bathing suits. But this is a decade before they will become my parents; they're two newlyweds, Richard and Michele, out on *Pippins.* The hull is painted white with a bright green stripe and the cabin gleams with fresh varnish. An American flag flies off the stern, and lobster buoys bob in their wake. Richard has one ropy arm around his pretty wife and the other on the tiller. Michele is wearing a pink bikini and her lips are coated in zinc. There is no land in sight. *Pippins* is immaculate.

I couldn't reconcile this evidence of a happy marriage existing between my parents. I'd grown so accustomed to thinking of my dad as the sole cause of my mom's rage and unhappiness that I didn't know what to make of these artifacts of my parents in better times, my parents in love, my mother pregnant with my brothers, and then with me, smiling for the camera with her hands on her belly, awaiting her New Year's Eve baby. It was 1985 by then.

We were living in Cape Cod, not far from the water, and all I remember about our first house was that a tree grew through the porch, and Dad hung a swing from it, and Mom rocked us in it whenever we cried. We moved to North Andover when I was three, and that's when things started to go bad.

When I ask my dad, years later, why they got divorced, he says it's impossible to answer. Still, he tries. Too young and immature, he'll say, in a committed if not hopeless kind of love. He realized that even though my mother was a pretty girl who liked to sail, the two of them didn't have all that much in common. He was quiet, serious, didn't drink. He wanted to make something of himself as an engineer. My mom was prone to emotional outbursts and Chardonnay. She'd had a difficult childhood that she was eager to put behind her by marrying young and starting her own family. Her mother drank too much, her sister had polio, her father died of a heart attack when she was sixteen, and her younger brother left for boarding school a year later. She met my dad two years after her father died, and he became a convenient way to start over.

He was handsome and he could fly. Obtaining his private pilot's license while in college, my dad owned a small airplane by the time Chris was born. He would fly us out to Martha's Vineyard for a day on the beach. He would fly us to tiny islands in the Bahamas, landing on grass strips where stray dogs milled about. He would fly us anywhere, playing the part in his Ray-Ban aviators and his green David Clark headset with its sleek black microphone. He radioed air-traffic controllers in a language I didn't understand, coded in shorthand and the phonetic alphabet. His hands worked the dashboard controls as if he were conducting an orchestra. We never worried with Dad as our pilot. Mom would soon be cut out of these trips entirely.

After a few years of married life, Dad was promoted to head engineer at Datamarine, a company that produced depth-finding devices. Mom was still moving between jobs while taking care of their three young children. Eventually she would find herself teaching special education, a career that fit well into her preferred caretaker role, although the pay wasn't great and dealing with the students' behavioral issues was often draining.

But before all that, before she needed more people to take care of, I was still a toddler and we were still living in that strange modern house on the Cape. One night my dad came home from work and tried to tell his wife that marriage was supposed to be more. There should be something for them to talk about other than their kids and their boat at the end of the day. Mom started yelling and all chance of an intelligent conversation went out the window. She was quick to get defensive, proud, and emotional. She must have been terrified of another imminent abandonment—first her father and now her husband. Stubborn to a fault, she would rather hold on to a bad thing than let it go completely. Dad was just as quick to grow silent, sullen, and withdrawn, which only stoked her anger. She felt rejected and he felt stuck. Neither would consider couples' therapy, where they would've had to endure the shame of displaying their shortcomings to a stranger. If my parents had anything in common, it was their pride: easily wounded and slow to heal.

They tried to make it work for a total of fifteen years. As the fights got louder, their vows disintegrated. There was no for better or for worse—it was all getting worse. Dad moved out right after we relocated to North Andover. It was 1988, and the divorce battle was under way. Lawyers were hired and the lines were drawn. Mom was so wounded by my dad wanting out of the marriage that the only way she saw to get back at him was by fighting for sole custody of my brothers and me. Dad owned a share of the high-tech company he was working for, and Mom received a large settlement. Even so, she got lawyers to seize his bank accounts, force him into depositions, and request endless paperwork. We didn't need more money. Mom was just trying to get back at Dad by playing the custody card. Dad continued to fight for visitation rights, but the most he ever got was permission to take my brothers and me out to dinner once a week and have us over to his house every other weekend.

On the day their divorce became official, Mom traded in our minivan for a Saab 900 Turbo. She also started wearing a big diamond ring, and even though I didn't ask, I knew it was a gift she'd bought herself.

As kids there seemed little point in discussing our parents' divorce when we were surrounded by its ongoing drama. When Dad would drive us home from Tuesday-night dinners, Mom would sometimes send me back out to his car to ask him for the child-support check. I hated being the messenger. His response was usually something along the lines of "Tell your mother she already took all my money," but I had a hard time understanding why he couldn't just write that magic check to appease her. I couldn't understand that it wasn't really about the money.

My brothers and I spent most of our time with Mom. She often found excuses to load us into the car and go for a drive at Dad's appointed pick-up times. It was difficult to see anything wrong with this, because Mom always spoiled us while Dad had the one-activity-per-weekend rule. On the weekends that we spent with him, we had to choose between the soccer game, birthday party, and friend's house. Dad's reasoning was that he wanted to spend more time with us, but Mom interpreted his rule as further evidence of bad parenting skills. All I knew was that I didn't want to choose—not between the activities, and not between my parents.

But despite all my worrying, most of the time my brothers and I had a lot of fun being shuttled back and forth. Our weekends with Dad felt like camping. We slept in sleeping bags and ate junk food. There was the time Dad put laundry detergent in the dishwasher and flooded the kitchen with bubbles. The time he hung Brad's socks on the chandelier to dry and they burst into flames. The time we rode a mattress down the stairs right when the landlord arrived. Back home on Sunday evenings, Mom would make us drink our milk and eat all our vegetables before leaving the dinner table. If she asked how our weekend was, my brothers and I might just smile at one another and say it was okay.

The photo album's thirty-year-old Polaroids of my mom could have been snapshots of me: the same hazel-eyed squint, dark tangled hair, and freckled shoulders. Even the curves of my legs seemed a direct inheritance. The photos also confirmed the uncanny resemblance between Brad and Dad. The same side-swept dark hair, prominent eyebrows, and smile that verged on a smirk. Kodachromed DNA.

The pictures of *Pippins* transported me. Our sailboat was the idea I loved most in the world, second only to my mom. One seemed an extension of the other.

The way we slept was the only thing I could remember of Dad being aboard, before my parents split and Mom claimed *Pippins* as her own. My bed was a piece of yellow foam on the cabin floor between their bunks. I closed my eyes to the sound of halyards clanking against masts, the boats around us rocking in their slips. I slept tucked in blankets with Dad snoring on my right, Mom's foot jutting out of her sleeping bag on my left, and my two brothers whispering in the bow.

After the divorce, Mom covered the navy blue cushions with nautical charts of the Atlantic, unfolding the Bermuda Triangle where Dad's sleeping bag had been. I continued to sleep on the floor. I couldn't bring myself to clear Dad's bunk. The nautical charts were heavy in their thick plastic sleeves, zipped safe from the salt that corroded everything else.

We docked *Pippins* at a boatyard in Wickford, Rhode Island, where Mom's younger brother George was the manager. He allowed Chris, Brad, and me free rein at the boatyard. We climbed into luggage carts and pushed each other up and down the docks. On Sunday mornings we raided the office for Honey Dew Donuts. During low tide we ran around with nets to scrape starfish from the pilings by the dinghy dock. Most nights for dinner, Mom gave us money to buy chicken salad and rolls at Ryan's Market. We hopped on our bikes and raced each other over the green metal bridge, making a right into town, which consisted of a main street lined with the drugstore, the grocer, and the fish market.

If the wind was blowing, we woke early and motored out of the harbor. Just before the breakwall, Mom took the helm and we scampered around the deck, cranking the winch and hoisting the sails. The lines pulled taut as *Pippins* dipped to the windward side. I was secretly terrified that our boat would capsize if the wind puffed one more breath into the bulging sail.

We floated by Fox Island and fishermen who sometimes waved and sometimes didn't. Past the island stood the abandoned lighthouse, all rust and bird droppings. Gulls squawked and smashed their catch against the rocks as we passed. Their chorus faded as we glided under the concrete ribs of the Jamestown Bridge. I held my breath on every passage, fearing that the mast would hit the bridge, get stuck, and push us under. Cars flew softly overhead. Mom steered with one hand draped lazily over the tiller, her bare feet propped on the cushions. She was much freer on the water, as if the wind carried her away from worrying about all the things that plagued her in North Andover. Give my mom a boat and she would become the captain, the crew, the photographer, the sandwich maker, the navigator, and the one to drop anchor for a swim at any enticing stretch of sea. She was invincible out there. During the summer, we often didn't see Dad for weeks. But when Mom was happy, it was infectious, and we didn't want to be anywhere other than out to sea with her.

On breezeless days, we motored *Pippins* to the outer harbor and went swimming. While my brothers and I inched down the swim ladder to test the water, Mom would strip to her black one-piece bathing suit and dive over our heads, toes pointed and arms extended. She was the first one in every time. She glided underwater and surfaced yards from the boat. Floating up toes first, she reclined as if in a lounge chair. She squinted the salt out of her eyes and we waited for her to say what she always said.

"Phew—beautiful!"

Chris, Brad, and I climbed atop the varnished cabin. We hoisted ourselves up onto the boom, accounting for its lurch and sway by making our own movements just as fluid. We steadied ourselves on the mast long enough to bend our knees and shout, "Mom, watch this!"

Then we jumped, the boom rocking back from under our feet as we flailed through the air without any of her grace, stinging our limbs as we belly flopped into the tepid harbor.

"Phew. Be-you-tee-ful!" we shouted upon surfacing.

Taking *Pippins* out of the water at the end of each August meant a return to land, another school year, and an otherwise unmagical existence in suburban Massachusetts. Back to the every-other-weekend shenanigans. We stood on deck as Mom motored the boat out of our slip on D Dock, past the dinghy dock, and over to the travel lift. Canvas slings hung from a blue metal frame, which rolled out on tracks above the water on four giant wheels.

I sometimes got to drive the travel lift while sitting on Uncle George's lap. I clutched his thick fingers as they pushed and pulled the ancient-looking knobs and gears. We lifted *Pippins* high enough to keep her green belly safe from scraping the ground. Metal stands wrapped with rags and duct tape stood waiting to shoulder the load. In the early years, *Pippins* was dry-docked inside the maintenance building, shielded from the rain and snow. We set her atop the stands, where she would hibernate like some strange bird on spindly legs for the winter.

After moving out of our house in North Andover, Dad took up residence in a one-bedroom apartment next to a 7-Eleven just across the New Hampshire border. Mom drove us there on alternate Friday evenings, and we all grew quiet as the neon 7-Eleven sign came into view. Saying good-bye was a drawn-out affair. After she left, though, we had a grand old time with Dad. Because his cooking skills were limited, dinner was often hot dogs and Slurpees from

7-Eleven. My dad would rest his hand atop mine as I pulled the sticky metal Slurpee dispenser, releasing it just before the cherry slush pooled out of the cup. Dad quickly became the favorite parent for the weekend. Allegiance was always shifting; I could be won over with dessert or a later bedtime.

After a few months by the convenience store, Dad moved into a duplex only five minutes away from us. Tuesday nights he took us out to dinner at Bertucci's or the Ninety Nine. Bertucci's had raw pizza dough to play with, while the Ninety Nine had free popcorn and Mountain Dew on tap: a tough choice. At Bertucci's we had the same waiter for at least a decade. Tony wore shorts all winter and always remembered our drink orders. I wondered if he could tell that my parents were divorced or if he thought Dad was a widower. But I could hardly tell Tony that my mother was home alone, most likely eating a microwaved dinner in front of the TV and peering out the window until we returned.

We stopped going to Bertucci's for a while after Chris and Brad decided to sneak their raw lumps of pizza dough outside after dinner one night and throw them at passing cars on Route 114. It was the first time I'd seen Dad get upset at anyone other than Mom. Unlike her outbursts when my brothers and I were misbehaving, Dad's anger was more like disappointment, cutting deeper than the string of revoked privileges that Mom often yelled up the stairs. Dad drove us back to Mom's and we scrambled out of the car, up the walkway, and into the house. Even though I hadn't thrown any dough myself, I felt implicated by my brothers' actions, as if we were one person bouncing between our two parents.

Tuesday-night dinners continued, but we started going to Wickford less frequently once my brothers and I reached adolescence. We were too busy with school, sports, and neighborhood paper routes to make the two-hour drive. It seemed foolish for Mom to varnish the cabin at the expense of her knees (the chemicals soaked through her jeans and bleached her skin as she crawled along the deck). There wasn't much sense in putting *Pippins* in the water anymore; sailing a thirty-foot boat by herself would not be easy or enjoyable. As our lives became landlocked, *Pippins* was moved to the back corner of the boatyard to bare its paint-chipped belly to the elements. The years went by and sailing became a thing of my past. But when I thought of *Pippins*, it wasn't sitting behind a shed. Our old wooden boat was moored in the harbor, and I was about to dive from the boom to the water, where my mother was waiting for me.

Chapter Eight

AFTER A FEW years in the duplex, Dad moved one last time to Beverly Farms. I was ten years old, and it was around this time that he met his second Michele. Just as he and Michele (Number One, my mother) had built their relationship around the restoration of a sailboat, Dad and Michele (Number Two, his girlfriend) got to know each other by renovating an old mansion turned boarding school. My brothers and I resented sharing what little time we had with our dad with someone else. Michele didn't seem very fun. Dad was suddenly yelling at us for things he'd found amusing before—like riding mattresses down the stairs—and we knew it was because Michele disapproved of our antics and told him so.

Michele was twelve years younger than Dad. My mom called her all kinds of names I'd never heard before, and in this way, I learned that being nice to my dad's girlfriend would mean betraying allegiance to my best friend. I never thought to question how my mom could condemn someone she had never met.

My brothers and I did everything we could to drive Michele away. We played pranks on her and poked her eyes out of photographs. We would have been little devil kids no matter whom Dad brought home. Michele's reserved manner didn't help, but then again, we didn't give her much to warm up to. We went home to our mom on Sunday nights, boasting that we would get rid of Dad's girlfriend soon enough.

But Michele stuck around, and for reasons unknown to us, Dad lit up like a bare bulb in her presence. Just as we began to worry that we might be stuck with her indefinitely, Dad announced over dinner that he was going to marry her. We were at Chili's, having exhausted the menus at both Bertucci's and the Ninety Nine. Our tacos got cold while we begged Dad to reconsider.

Mom was not going to like this.

It wasn't that she was hoping to get back together with our father. It was more that she resented him for being able to do what she could not. With a full-time teaching job and three kids, Mom didn't have a whole lot of time to date. She spent her afternoons helping her aging mother and picking my brothers and me up from soccer practice. She had a few close friends, but as I would later learn, she stopped returning their phone calls around the time she moved to Newburyport.

Dad and Michele married on the Fourth of July, 1996. They said their vows before a small gathering of friends and relatives by the bay window in the living room. Misery Island was dark and jagged on the horizon. Brad refused to take part in the ceremony and ran off to hide in the limbs of the giant beech tree beside the house. I was enjoying my role as the flower girl, spreading petals in my wake, but then there was my guilt, and I wondered what my mom was doing. The best fireworks show around was right in Dad's front yard, where a barge moored off the rocks lit up the sky for Independence Day to a packed beach after the sun went down. I couldn't wait.

I was a freshman in high school when my dad and Michele announced that they were having a baby. I'd recently entered into what my dad called my "bold phase." I refused to go to the hospital, telling Dad over the phone that he was too old to be a father (he was approaching fifty) and that Michele would make a horrible mother. I said lots of things I didn't really mean, but since my mom had said them I figured they were true. That this was Dad's second chance to not be such a screwup, that he would love the baby more than my brothers and me. That he was out of touch with reality, holed up in his mansion with his new wife and his new kid.

Chris and Brad didn't seem to share my constant fear of disappointing Mom. They knew when she was being petty and told her so. While I had always tried to please both parents—this meant my mom on a daily basis, and my dad only on Tuesday nights and alternating weekends—Chris and Brad tended to do whatever they thought was right. Because their allegiance was never a given, my brothers maintained solid footing with both parents.

After Maggie was born, Dad sewed a flag out of pink felt and hung it on the flagpole by the beach. Although I was jealous of the baby getting so much of his attention, I started driving over to

Beverly more often, intrigued by Maggie's enormous blue eyes and tiny fingers. My dad hadn't always been there when I was little, and while it stung, it was also illuminating to see him parenting around the clock now that he had retired. Maggie hardly ever cried, and Dad seemed like a kid himself, cradling her in his arms as he sung made-up lullabies. Maybe this *was* his second chance. But even if my mom told me to, I couldn't hold it against him if he wanted to make the most of it.

If I made the mistake of mentioning my new sister around my mom, she'd say, "You mean your *half* sister." It was true that we looked nothing alike—me with almost-black hair and sharp features, Maggie blond and button-nosed—but I couldn't help loving her completely, as a sister. I was starting to see how selfish it was of my mom to ask me to keep my distance from a little girl, simply because she came from another woman.

College was going to be my escape: no more choosing sides. Brown was two hours south, just far enough to be far enough. I was accepted early, and Mom drove four hours round-trip to buy me pencils, decals, a coffee mug, a key chain, and a sweatshirt from the campus bookstore, all of which she wrapped and placed under the tree on Christmas morning. I crawled into the trunk of her car and stuck the Brown University sticker across the back window. She relished the proud parent role.

A few months before I left for college, Mom announced that she was going to sell our house. My brothers and I weren't all that attached to North Andover and we were excited for Mom to get a fresh start somewhere else. The four of us cleaned, painted, labeled boxes, laughed, sweated, and spent a lot of time together that summer.

Along with an old accordion, an inflatable canoe, and stiff canvas sail bags, we found good old Richard in the basement. Richard was a life-sized dummy that Mom had bought after her divorce and jokingly named after our father. He had a full head of salt-and-pepper hair, waxen cheeks with an airbrushed five o'clock shadow, and big blue doll eyes. Mom sometimes strapped him into the passenger seat so she could use the carpool lane during rush hour. Richard was outfitted in suit and tie, his wardrobe compliments of a neighbor whose husband hadn't bothered to empty his closet before leaving. He sat in front of the kitchen window whenever we went away for the weekend. Mom didn't want anyone to know there wasn't a man of the house.

We carried Richard from the basement to the Dumpster in the driveway. When we had a yard sale, we made sure he was fully covered with trash bags. We wouldn't want anyone thinking they saw a dead body in our trash.

At the end of August we packed up the car and Mom drove me down to Providence for my freshman orientation. She stayed long after she had met my roommate and helped me unpack. Finally we stood outside my dorm and said our good-byes. I tried not to get emotional, but my lungs fought for air the second she rounded the corner and drove out of sight.

I returned home a few months later because our house had sold. There was a moving truck to fill and a storage unit to rent. All it took was a U-Haul, a FOR SALE sign, and my brothers to lift the heavy stuff. Another family would make our rooms their own and it would be as if we'd never been there.

Mom rented a one-bedroom apartment in Newburyport. We didn't have any friends or relatives there, but being near the water seemed a necessity. For all I knew, she could have chosen where to move by gliding her finger across a map of New England and stopping at the first place where green became blue. She seemed primed for a fresh start, and as we transported her belongings, we were not too worried.

A few weeks later, when I next saw her, she was driving a white Subaru Outback. Her new station wagon reminded me of our old minivan: good for car seats and little kids, neither of which Mom had anymore.

I took the train up to visit her almost every weekend that first semester of college, and I wasn't always sure whether it was because I was lonely or she was. All I knew was that things felt better when we were together, and instead of trying to make my own friends at school, I just wanted to hang out with her. We'd go out to eat, go shopping, walk on the beach, make cocktails. It didn't ever matter what we were doing—as long as we weren't arguing, we were finishing each other's sentences.

But as the school year wore on, I became less homesick and started spending more time with Cassidy, experiencing college life on the weekends instead of fleeing. My mom still called me a few times a day, a frequency I didn't find abnormal. If I said I had to go, she'd get offended and more or less hang up on me. And then I'd call her right back.

By my sophomore year, I liked college and was looking forward to returning from my long winter break. My twentieth birthday fell on New Year's Eve, and I wanted to spend it with friends in Providence. I was at my uncle George's ski cabin in Vermont with my brothers, my mom, my uncle, and my cousin Kelsey. I didn't want to spend another New Year's playing Monopoly and going to bed long before midnight.

I asked my mom if Kelsey and I could drive to Providence for the night and return the next day. She said no, claiming there'd be too many drunk drivers on the road.

"And don't you want to spend your birthday with the one who brought you into this world?"

She said this like it were a debt that I could never fully repay. If I stayed by her side at all times, then I could at least cut down the accruing interest.

"We'll drive back up tomorrow," I said.

"Just stay here."

Switching tack from the vetoed Providence plan, Kelsey and I asked if we could spend a girls' night at my mom's apartment in Newburyport instead. Kelsey was three years younger and practically my sister; George could never say no to his only daughter, who lived with her mother in Florida and came up to visit only a few times a year. Besides, I could tell that he didn't see what the big deal was, and we talked him into letting us borrow his car for the night.

Although her apartment was a three-hour drive from the ski cabin, Mom seemed to have forgotten about her drunk-driver argument. Her logic didn't always carry from one situation to the next.

"Fine, go. Obviously you don't want to be with me."

George fished his car keys out of his coat pocket, tossed them to Kelsey, and we were on our way. We bypassed the Newburyport exit on I-95 and continued on to Providence. Arriving at my dorm around dinnertime, we met up with a few friends who'd stuck around for the holidays and promptly uncorked a bottle of cheap champagne.

Brad somehow knew that Kelsey and I were never planning on going to Mom's apartment for a quiet evening of movies and manicures. Deciding it'd be more entertaining to trap me in my lie rather than tell Mom where I really was, he devised a plan and told Mom to call me at eight. I shouldn't have answered, but I always answered when she called.

"Hey, Linds, I need a favor. Can you deliver the rent check to the landlord down the street? It's on the kitchen table, I forgot to mail it," she said.

"Can it wait till tomorrow?"

"No, today's the last day of the month. It'll take you five minutes."

"I can't do it tonight."

"Why not?"

"Because I'm too far away."

I confessed. She called me a liar and hung up. I tried to make the best of my remaining hours of freedom—dancing on the roof of a parking garage as snow swirled and fireworks exploded—but I ended the night and entered my twenties spewing champagne into a toilet.

Mom must have left Vermont in the wee hours of the morning because she was honking outside my dorm at eight a.m. on New Year's Day. Kelsey would take her dad's car, while I was left to face my mom alone.

I climbed into the passenger seat. Mom didn't say hi, or happy

New Year, or anything at all. She wouldn't look at me. She popped the clutch and pushed up through the gears, first to fifth. I buckled my seat belt. We shot onto the highway going at least eighty, weaving in and out of the fast lane. Painfully hungover, I clamped my mouth shut in an attempt to settle my stomach. Throwing up in Mom's new car would give her one more thing to hold against me. Plow trucks cleared the freshly fallen snow, spitting sand in their wake. My head pulsed. Our Outback was the fastest-moving car on the road.

Her face revealed nothing. I ventured an apology, hoping it would help her find the brake pedal.

"I'm sorry I lied, but I think I deserve a little independence. I'm twenty, not fourteen."

"You think you're too good for me? We'll see how you like living with your father and paying for your car insurance, and your gas, and everything else you never thank me for, and don't come crying to me when you want something."

"That's not what I said. I said I was sorry."

"Nope, you're done with me. So I'm done with you."

"Mom, I'm sorry!"

I spent the rest of the ride home apologizing, but it was no use. She acted as if I wasn't even in the car, as if there wasn't a layer of snow covering the road. It was the angriest I'd ever seen her, but like all our arguments, I figured it would blow over within an hour. I was practically crying, but her emotions were contained, which was even more alarming. Other than the speedometer jagging up to ninety miles per hour, there was no sign of her rage. I thought her tendency to flip from angry overbearing mother to my best friend again was perfectly normal. I just had to ride out her fury along with my hangover. We'd be hugging and making up by dinnertime, and with any luck, my pounding headache would be gone by then too.

We parked outside her apartment and climbed the stairs.

"Pack your stuff. I don't have all day," she said.

Not until she handed me a box of trash bags did I realize she was serious. Banishment seemed too harsh a punishment for standard teenage rebellion, but I figured she just wanted to make me feel guilty for lying to her. I kept wondering when she would give in. But she didn't even take off her coat. She paced around with car keys in hand until I'd balled up some clothing into a few trash bags. It was as if all emotion had drained out of her, leaving a coldhearted stranger disguised as my mother. An hour later, she was dropping me at the door of my dad's house and hurling my belongings out of the trunk.

"This is what you wanted," she said as she left.

I stood amid plastic bags full of jeans and sweaters, feeling as if I'd just been tossed out of my lifeboat.

I blinked back tears as I entered the kitchen, where Dad and Michele were standing, as if on cue.

"What happened?" Dad said.

"Mom got mad at me."

"Why?"

"Kelsey and I wanted to go to Providence for New Year's Eve and she wouldn't let us. We borrowed George's car and went anyway. Now she thinks I don't want anything to do with her and told me to come live with you."

"Do you expect me to say I'm surprised?"

"What do you mean?"

"You've needed to stand up to your mother for years."

"I just wanted to go out with my friends."

"Which is totally normal."

"You did the right thing," Michele interjected.

"I've never seen her this mad at me."

"She'll get over it."

But I wasn't so sure anymore.

I spent the next three weeks at my father's house. Even though the house had a dozen bedrooms, Dad turned on the thermostat in only one wing during the winter, and I shared a room with Maggie during the cold months. Dad suggested jackets and hats to anyone who complained of the cold. Despite the double-paned storm windows, a winter draft still found its way in.

I'd rarely spent more than a weekend at a time at his house. Anytime he saw me pacing the halls with my cell phone pressed to my ear, Dad would say, "Don't give in," as if he knew I was calling my mom, ready to beg forgiveness, if only she would answer.

I didn't want to be congratulated for inadvertently severing ties with her. I spent the rest of January trying to figure out how twenty years of unwavering allegiance had been trumped by one stupid fight, one little lie. She'd always been annoyingly stubborn, but she'd never held out on me for this long before. How many times would I have to say I was sorry?

I distracted myself by playing with Maggie. I peeled off my socks and stuck my feet in her bubble bath every night, making a bridge of my legs for her to swim under. She was thrilled that her big sister was staying for more than the usual twenty-four hours. The days passed in limbo, the nights under electric blankets.

At the end of the month, Dad drove me back to Providence for my second semester. I had never been around my dad so much and talked to my mom so little.

"She'll call eventually," he said as we pulled up to my dorm.

"Thanks for letting me stay at your house."

"It's your home too."

"Bye, Dad."

I grabbed my bags out of the trunk and walked through the brick archway to the quad. It was a relief to return to Cassidy, and classes, and some sense of what it was supposed to be like to be a sophomore in college. Except that all I could think about was how messy things had become between my mom and me, and how I was to blame. Although I wasn't sure why, apologizing didn't seem to be enough to get us back to the way we'd always been: like two halves of the same needy person.

When she finally called at the beginning of February, I answered the phone ready to launch into my most earnest and prolonged apology. Five weeks had passed since our argument; if independence meant not talking to her, it wasn't worth it. But she brushed aside my apology and asked whether I'd be free the following afternoon to sign some papers. I was so happy to hear from her that I didn't bother to ask what needed my signature. I was used to never-mention-it mediation, and if my mom wanted to act as if New Year's Eve hadn't happened, that was fine by me. I said she could come down anytime the next day. We settled on four o'clock. She'd be coming directly from work.

She was idling at the curb outside my dorm the next afternoon, right on time. I got in the passenger seat and leaned over to hug her. She looked past me as she pulled back from a limp, formal embrace, nothing like the bear hugs we usually shared.

She reached into the backseat as I sat waiting for her to make eye contact. But she was as detached as she had been on New Year's. I couldn't tell whether I was forgiven but we'd never go back to the way we were, or if she was still so angry that she couldn't even look at me. Her complexion looked doughy, her drugstore foundation oily from its morning application. Mauve lipstick ringed her mouth, same as always. The Subaru still had that new car smell: a blend of upholstery, plastic, and a dentist's office sterility.

She swept her arm around behind her, feeling her way over the floor, the backseat, and the center console. A rustle of papers, and her hand appeared again with a red folder, which she dropped onto my lap. She released the emergency brake and pulled onto the street. ESTATE PLANNING OF MICHELE V. HARRISON was typed on a white label on the front of the folder.

"What's this?"

"Just some documents."

"Estate planning?"

"It's no big deal—everyone my age makes a will."

"A will? Are you sick? What's wrong?"

"Nothing. I'm fine."

"I'm not signing anything until you promise me you're okay."

"I'm fine, Lindsay, don't be difficult. The documents are for your own good."

We drove down George Street, turned right onto Benefit, and left onto Angell, coasting down steep potholed hills. We crossed the Providence River by way of a two-lane bridge, the water stagnant and a string of empty fire pits hovering above the surface like abandoned birds' nests. A few times a year the city lit the pits at dusk and let them burn through the night. Little kids in face paint ran around fisting giant orbs of cotton candy while their parents bought beer from harried vendors and listened to local bands. They called it WaterFire. I'd gone the year before at Halloween but thought it too crowded and hokey.

Mom pulled up outside the Bank of America building, a stately columned affair a few blocks past the river.

"They should have a notary. I'll wait out here," she said.

"You're serious?"

"I can't park here so I'll circle the block. Hurry up."

I tucked the folder under my arm and walked into the bank. I reached for my cell phone and called Brad to ask whether he knew about the documents.

"She's making a trust," he said.

"You knew about this?"

"Yeah."

"It seems sketchy to me."

"Just sign it. She's doing it for us, in case anything happens to her."

The notary motioned for me to follow him into his office. The sound of his shoes striking the marble floor echoed up to the vaulted ceiling. I began to sweat in my heavy winter coat.

He flipped through the documents and told me where to sign, offering a black ballpoint. I was too flustered to read what I was signing. All I knew was that there were three copies with dotted lines. I signed my name in all the right places, not at all sure that I was doing the right thing. Then the notary stamp bit into the pages, once, twice, three times, and I was ushered back out to the lobby, where I exited the revolving doors and stepped onto the sidewalk.

Mom's Subaru was crawling up the block. A light rain had begun to fall, despite the sun slanting through the clouds. Across the street, a wrecking ball was poised for another pass at an old building the city was destroying. All that remained was the back wall, its windows already blown out. On what must've been the second floor, a lone set of French doors reflected the sunlight as they stood waiting to take the hit. I forgot about the red folder clutched in my hands long enough to wish I had my camera with me. Order, pattern, and composition: I longed for a world that could fit on a filmstrip.

Mom pulled up to the curb and I got back in the car.

"Here. I signed it."

"Need any groceries?" she asked, tossing the folder onto the backseat.

I didn't answer.

We drove back up College Hill, passing campus and turning toward the grocery store on the east side of Providence. The red folder, like the New Year's fight, was another thing that we apparently weren't going to talk about. I knew Mom was offering to buy me groceries as some kind of bargain for my silence. I was wary of another argument and told her where to turn. We walked through the sliding doors in silence. She pushed a cart while I wandered the produce section and bagged some apples.

All of a sudden Mom checked her watch, saw that it was almost five o'clock, and thrust her credit card at me. She said something about getting to the post office before it closed. I knew she'd come pick me up when she was done, but I was so annoyed that she left me there that I walked the twenty minutes back to campus. I was approaching my dorm when she pulled up and rolled down the window.

"I had to overnight the documents to Brad before the post office closed," she said.

I handed her Visa through the window and turned away. She was calling my name but I didn't turn around. Everything felt inverted, my vision distorting perspective as I crossed the street and passed through the gate leading to my dorm. Once I had rounded the corner, I dropped the grocery bags and bent forward, my hands on my hips and my eyes shut tight. Ever since New Year's my eyes had been spinning me into vertigo. For a few minutes it felt like I was falling into a black hole, and then all of a sudden, I was fine again.

My mom and I lapsed back into not speaking. I busied myself with schoolwork while she looked at real estate in New Hampshire. I heard about all this from my brothers, who said that Mom felt bad about not having space for us in her small apartment and wanted a house where we could have our own bedrooms again.

Three weeks later, at the beginning of March, Mom phoned to ask if she could take me out to dinner. I wanted my best friend back, and if the only way to reach her was to never mention the red folder, or New Year's Eve, or any of it, I could live with that.

I met her outside my dorm the next night. I had no idea what kind of terms we were on. She fixed her eyes on me. They were greener than I'd remembered. Her mouth was lacquered up in an eager smile. She gave me a quick hug across the gearshift.

"Buckle up," she said.

We ate at the Cheesecake Factory in downtown Providence. I ordered pasta and she got seafood. I could feel the rift between us and tried to fill it by talking about my classes and my summer plan to land a photography job someplace more exciting than Massachusetts.

"Why don't you want to live with me?" she asked.

"You could visit."

My mom couldn't help but see every choice I made as something that would either bring me closer or farther away.

I wanted to talk about what had happened on New Year's, but I could tell that I'd upset her again without meaning to. Why would I move someplace random when I could move back to Newburyport and spend all summer with her? She expected me to remain tethered to her indefinitely.

I changed topics, asking her about the houses she'd been scouting with a Realtor. She said she'd found the perfect one and was hoping to close on it within the week.

"What's it like?" I asked.

"You'll have to wait and see."

"I can come up on my spring break in a few weeks."

Just then the fire alarm went off in the restaurant, making it impossible to hear her response. She paid the bill and we zipped our coats, heading out to the parking garage and driving back up to my dorm. I would see her soon, I was sure of it. I'd take the train up for the weekend and drive to the mountains to see this new house of hers. I would stop saying sorry and just try to be a better daughter. We would only move forward.

I turned to wave as I walked toward my dorm, my breath steaming in the crisp cold night, lit not by stars but by Christmas lights still strung between dorm windows. My mother pulled into the street and it was too dark to tell whether she was waving back. And just like that I lost her.

Chapter Nine

I WOKE ONE MORNING in October feeling as if my lungs were collapsing. I was covered in clammy sweat. My chest was in a vise. I swung my legs off the side of my creaky dorm mattress. I stepped into my torn Levi's and pulled a hooded sweatshirt over the green T-shirt I'd slept in. The front featured a dog running around a pine tree, and the back read HAVE A REAL TREE. MERRY CHRISTMAS. Cassidy and I had been trading it back and forth for so long that I couldn't remember whose it was. I grabbed my keys and walked out of the dorm, considering the likelihood of a heart attack at the age of twenty.

It was my first fall without my mom and all I could think of was the trips we used to take to New Hampshire, driving crooked back roads and photographing foliage. *Leaf-peeping trips.* We'd stop at farm stands for glass bottles of milk. It was hard to be back at school, hard to be a junior.

I hunched forward and walked over to the quad where I'd lived with Cassidy the year before. Everything felt sharp in a way it hadn't since my summer night in the Maine hospital. The campus sliced into me like shards of a broken bottle, my breath catching on every inhalation.

I entered the health center and complained of chest pains to the receptionist. A nurse bustled out to escort me to a cramped examining room on the third floor. She handed me a paper gown and said she'd be right back. I peeled off my clothes. Climbing onto the table, I was grateful for the crinkling paper beneath me, which kept my bare legs from shivering like they had on the sterilized metal at the hospital three months earlier. A poster of a tropical beach was tacked to the fiber-paneled ceiling.

The nurse returned pushing a rolling cart loaded with what appeared to be a giant fax machine, a tangle of wires dangling behind.

"Try to relax," she said.

My jaw was clenched and the scabs on my thumbs were freshly cracked.

"Has anything been causing you stress lately?" she asked.

"My mom died six months ago, so I guess there's that."

"Oh, I'm so sorry, honey! Did she have cancer?"

They were always sorry, these strangers. And they always assumed it was cancer, as if a virus gnawing away at her insides would have somehow softened the blow or left me better prepared for the ending.

"No, not cancer. She just died."

I couldn't talk about it. The nurse was holding a file of my school records and I knew it was all in there anyway. My heart was expanding like a balloon ready to burst and I looked at the machine in an effort to hurry the pleasant woman along.

She untangled the wires and plugged in the electrocardiogram machine.

"This might be cold, hon."

I wore the gown with the slit in the front, pulling it open to bare my pale midriff. The nurse hummed as she rubbed a clear liquid around my breasts, attaching electrodes and wires on top. I stared at the poster on the ceiling. What came to mind was not a Caribbean beach but all the times my old Saab had stalled out and needed a jump start. Mom would come meet me wherever I was stranded and run jumper cables from her car to mine, until one current became two.

I'd never had an EKG before. With my chest covered in wires, I waited for an electrical shock of some kind, a jolt to reset my heartbeat. Cold sweat began to pool in my armpits. I was still waiting for something to happen when the nurse said, "Honey, you're all done. You can peel those off and get dressed while I print the results."

I wiped the goop off my chest with a paper towel and pulled on my clothes. A doctor came in holding a graph. I had no experience reading medical charts, but even I could see that my heart's activity was moving up and down in the most even of beats. I'd been expecting a printout that looked more like a seismogram after a major earthquake.

"Well, it's not a heart attack you're having."

"What is it, then?"

"Looks like an anxiety attack."

The doctor entered my data into the computer as she spoke

about grief being able to cause extreme physical pain. I was thinking only of the prescription for anti-anxiety medication that she was writing me. I filled it that afternoon, took two pills, and poured myself some rum, despite the warning on the bottle.

My chest cavity expanded as if I were exhaling for the first time in days. My fingers tingled as I stretched out on the carpet in my dorm room. Between the sorority and the religious dorm, no one would be looking for me, and I planned on staying in for a good long while. I knew I'd mix the pills with alcohol, just as I'd done with Prozac. Anything to forget faster.

The anxiety attack, the first of many, was the only thing I remember happening that fall. Mostly things didn't happen: I pulled away from the friends I'd shared a dorm with the year before. Along with my dad and brothers, my college friends called plenty. But listening to their messages saying it would be great to catch up at this or that night's party, I couldn't help but remember them huddled in the hallway the semester before, whispering about my drinking problem and voting on who should inform my dad about it. All of them had come to my mom's memorial, but still.

I didn't want to talk about what had happened but I couldn't keep up with small talk, either. If anyone asked, I'd say I was fine. This was college, after all. Everything was supposed to be casual, carefree, see you at the next party. And if you did care about something at Brown, you were supposed to set up a table on the Main Green and sell vegan cookies and hand out flyers. I floated from class to class, feeling wasted even when I wasn't.

December brought snow and I packed my bags for Christmas break. My brothers and I had always gone skiing with our mom for the holiday. Dad decided we should head south instead.

We flew to Florida on Christmas day to visit Dad's younger brother, our uncle John. The runny nose I boarded the plane with became a pounding sinus infection by the time we touched down in sunny Fort Lauderdale. We peeled off our layers and changed into shorts once we got to John's house in Pompano. I sat by the pool while Maggie splashed around, shielded from our sadness.

John captained boats for a living, chartering fancy yachts back and forth from the Caribbean. A hundred-foot powerboat was tied up at the dock behind his house, where the Intracoastal Waterway cut between backyards like a busy road. We'd be bunking on the boat for our stay. Dad, Michele, and Maggie went aboard by eight o'clock, tired from the day of travel.

Chris was in the house watching college football on TV. Brad and I stayed up late with John and our aunt Sharyn, drinking Budweisers on the porch overlooking the canal. The water was calm. No boats passed. Tiny white bulbs strung on palm trees reflected across the surface of the water like schools of phosphorescent fish.

By ten o'clock Brad had more than a few beer cans lined up in front of him. I was nursing number five.

We'd exhausted the safe topics of conversation: the weather, the holidays, and the latest antics of John's dog Boomer.

"How are you guys feeling about everything?" Sharyn asked.

The silence was interrupted only by intermittent pulls on our beer cans. We knew what she meant by *everything*. Brad and I hadn't discussed the missing person search or finding our mother since the boat ride back from Misery seven months earlier, when

I'd wondered aloud how any of it could have happened and he'd said not to ask.

Sharyn abruptly excused herself for bed, pulling John with her. "You two should talk," she said.

Maybe we needed someone to tell us as much. Maybe it was the beer, or the climate, or Christmas, or the distance between Massachusetts and Florida that allowed us to take the leap. Or maybe we just couldn't keep pretending there was nothing to say about everything.

I fiddled with the top of the nearest can, working the metal tab back and forth until it snapped. Brad started speaking, offering more than his usual one-word answers. He was saying that Mom had screwed him over. I thought the alcohol buzzing between my ears might've caused me to mishear.

"What are you talking about?" I asked.

"Mom told me she was thinking of killing herself."

"What?"

"I told you this the night she went missing. You just didn't want to hear it."

"No you didn't. Tell me now."

"When I talked to Mom a few days before she disappeared, she said she was thinking of killing herself and asked me how I'd do it."

"She asked you that?"

"Yeah, she called and woke me up. It was when I had mono."

"What'd you say to her?"

"I told her I'd never thought about it because I would never do that. I asked her why she'd even say something like that."

"And?"

"She said she was really stressed out."

"About what?"

"She wouldn't say."

"Stressed about buying the house in New Hampshire?"

"I guess. I don't know. I was wicked sick, I was half asleep."

"What else did she say?"

"That she'd be too 'chickenshit' to actually hurt herself. That she wouldn't know how to do it."

We fell quiet, looking anywhere but at each other. I was starting to think that having this conversation was a horrible idea. I didn't want to be hearing more that I couldn't make sense of. Brad's words were cracking me open, but I knew I had to see the conversation through.

"So the whole time she was missing, you basically knew we wouldn't find her alive?" I asked.

"No, I didn't think she was serious. You know how sometimes people say they're going to kill themselves?"

I knew exactly what he meant. It was a toxic phrase I heard all the time in her absence, from friends suffering from a slight annoyance or too much homework. But Mom had never talked about life as if it were disposable. Every now and then when my brothers and I got on her nerves, she'd say, "You'll be sorry when I'm gone." We would roll our eyes at the impossibility. But how right she had been. How sorry we were for having to talk about her in the past tense, for missing her so badly that we could hardly talk to each other about it. How sorry for everything.

"You definitely didn't tell me this before," I said.

"Yes I did! I told Chris, Dad, the police, everyone. When she first told me, I didn't believe it either. Didn't want to. I thought if we searched hard enough, we could find her before she did anything stupid."

"I can't believe she told you she was thinking of killing herself."

"It's not my fault, Lindsay."

"I wouldn't have known what to say either."

I chugged a few mouthfuls of beer. I wanted his words to evaporate. I hated imagining the conversation between my brother and my mother that had occurred right before she went missing. How Brad had mono, how Mom had caught him off guard. It was the last time they ever spoke. I was ripped apart all over again. How could she have said such a thing to her own son?

"And I helped her make that trust a few weeks before it happened. She promised me she was fine, said she just wanted help with the lawyer," he said.

Mom had made me the same promise. If only we had known not to believe her.

"You met with her lawyer?"

"I was trying to help."

"I knew that was sketchy. You told me it was normal, but she was in such a rush about the whole thing."

"Yeah, well, I never thought she'd screw us over like this."

We sat in silence, letting all that had come to pass settle. I couldn't believe I'd managed to repress such a pivotal conversation for so long. And I couldn't imagine the guilt Brad must be feeling about helping Mom make a trust two weeks before she ended her life.

"You didn't do anything wrong, Brad. I hope you know that," I said.

I could feel his eyes swimming toward me in the Southern darkness, but I couldn't talk or listen anymore. Christmas was not supposed to be like this.

I walked down to the dock, stepped aboard the boat, and crawled into my bunk. As I waited for sleep, I wondered whether I would ever understand the whole story, or whether missing someone meant that there would always be details you would long to know, conversations you'd wish you could better remember, and others' recollections that you would struggle to align with your own.

Grief could be like amnesia sometimes. After my conversation with Brad, though, there was a brittle new clarity to the unsavory details of my mother's forty-day disappearance. So much I'd chosen to cast aside, but now, nine months after she didn't show up for work, my memory was returning with full force. Alcohol couldn't quell the flashbacks anymore. Just like that, a certain night came slamming back to me, serving as proof that Brad had in fact told me of that conversation long before.

The parking garage.

It was the night she disappeared. While Chris and I were checking gas stations for security tapes, Brad called and told us to drive through any parking garages we could find around Newburyport. When I asked him why, he'd said something about carbon monoxide poisoning being a relatively easy way to go.

It was then that Brad relayed his last conversation with our mom to Chris and me. She'd told him she was thinking of killing herself, and now he was imagining ways she might do it.

Chris knew of a hotel with a parking garage a few exits north. We got back on I-95, and in the growing darkness, I was glad I couldn't see my brother's face. What Brad had just told us was impossible. Our mom wouldn't do that. Not to us. But still, we had to check.

We crawled up the ramp to a garage a few minutes later. Overhead lights cast a sinister orange glow over clusters of parked cars. We drove along the rows, looking for a white Subaru Outback while praying we wouldn't see one. We circled the mostly vacant first level and took another ramp up to the top floor of the lot. I held my breath as a white station wagon came into view up on the right. Chris slowed down and I knew he'd seen it too.

It was a Volvo, not a Subaru.

We scanned the last row and spiraled down the ramps and back out into the night to resume our gas station circuit.

"Mom would never do that," I said as soon as we were back on the highway.

"No way."

I got through the next forty days by convincing myself that suicide was not a possible outcome. I refused to let lost or found mean dead or alive. I willed Brad's parking garage theory to be untrue. Whenever fear started to override my hope, I reminded myself that there was simply no way Mom would cause my brothers and me that kind of irremediable pain.

But right from the start, Brad had warned me that this was, in fact, a possibility. So as bad as it was to relive that feeling of seeing a look-alike station wagon in the parking garage, it was even harder to accept that I had managed to submerge it for so long, mixing up the narrative like another liquor-and-pills night. Some part of me had known all along that we might not find our mother alive, but creeping through that garage was so sickening that I had no choice but denial and disremembering.

I should have shown Brad more sympathy on Christmas night, though. Not only had he led the search, made the call when our mother's body was found, and paid her overdue bills, but he'd also suspected from the beginning that those burdens would fall to him. All the time I'd spent hoping that Mom would come waltzing into her apartment, Brad had spent hoping that she was too *chickenshit* to act on her words.

We would never know where our mother was during those six weeks she was missing, what she was doing, or even how long she was alive in that time. And we would never know exactly why she'd said those words on the phone two nights before she disappeared. Our mom had become an unsolvable mystery. How were we supposed to cope with a loss whose very facts would always remain unknowable to us?

The week after we got back from Florida, I drove up to Vermont to visit Cassidy. She had just returned home from her semester in South Africa. I put my Jeep in four-wheel drive at the bottom of her snowed-over driveway. A half mile up, I crested over the final ridge and her house came into view, a white A-frame with a barn behind, both built by her father.

Cassidy came running through the snow. We hadn't seen each other in six months. In our weekly e-mail exchanges, she'd mentioned losing her appetite and feeling listless in Cape Town, but the girl running toward me was a shell of my best friend. I stopped the car and jumped out to hug her. I could feel her shoulder blades through her thick sweatshirt, but I didn't say anything.

Once inside and stripped of our bulky layers, I got a good look at her. The year before, we'd shared a closet in our dorm room, trading jeans and tank tops. But since I'd last seen her, it looked like she'd lost about forty pounds from her already lean five-eight frame. Her pants hung loose on her thighs, and I could see that she'd carved a few new notches into her old leather belt.

We talked late into the night about our semesters apart and how lonely they'd been. She was self-conscious about the weight she'd dropped and how everyone kept commenting on it. She'd lost her appetite halfway around the world and said eating even beans and rice had been a chore. Living with a bunch of Americans who wanted mainly to get stoned and party, Cassidy explored the city alone. Alcohol and drugs had never much appealed to her, and I loved her for seeing the emptiness in all that, especially because I couldn't.

A nagging voice in my head kept telling me that her deterioration was my fault. That living with me the year before had been so burdensome that it spiraled her toward a depression that caught up with her on another continent. She'd been more affected by my mother's death than I'd realized. Maybe it was partly that. But she had her own demons to fight and it was time for me to be the kind of friend she'd been to me all along.

By the end of January we were both back at school for the beginning of spring semester. Once a week Cassidy had to see a doctor who weighed her, accused her of being anorexic, and ordered her to drink Ensure. She was placed in a freshman dorm on the other side of campus, but one of us made the trek to see the other almost every night.

I knew I needed some kind of an outlet for everything that was roiling inside me. I couldn't dump all my sorrows on Cassidy when she was in her own precarious state. At the beginning of the school year I'd received an invitation in my e-mail, which I'd ignored for months. I dug it up again: the Brown Bereavement Group, hosted by the university chaplain, meetings on Fridays at five p.m. I didn't like the thought of sitting around with a bunch of depressed students while everywhere else on campus the first round of drinks was being poured, but I was desperate.

Parties, my dorm room, the dining hall, and even the library were all becoming difficult places to be on a Friday night. When I finally dragged myself to the bereavement group, it was with the hope that my emotions wouldn't be as incongruous there as they seemed to be everywhere else.

So with Cassidy's pep talk ringing in my ears, I walked up the stairs in the student center, trying to find the room mentioned on the invite. The basement housed the post office, while the main floor featured a bakery whose muffins weren't doing me any favors. I'd never been up to the second floor. I held on to the banister. A sign was tacked to the first door in a long hallway of offices: BEREAVEMENT GROUP MEETS HERE AT 5. I kept walking, trying to look like I was going somewhere else, hoping there was another set of stairs at the other end of the hallway, down which I could make my escape. But a woman with short silver hair popped her head out of the doorway.

"Hi, I'm Janet," she called out. "Come in. We've got cookies!"

I turned around as if in slow motion, cursing myself for wearing my wooden-heeled boots, so clunky she must have heard me coming. I was trapped.

Six faces mooned up at me from a circle of chairs. The office wasn't cluttered with crucifixes as I'd imagined. It was a sprawling room, with Oriental rugs, towering paned windows facing the Main Green, and soft yellow light spilling from goosenecked lamps in the corners. I sat on the edge of an upholstered chair, my eyes darting from one face to the next, trying to size up each one's tragedies. They seemed just as unsure as I was of how to respond to Janet's banter, which flowed out in a stream of random anecdotes while she freighted mismatched coffee mugs and chocolate chip cookies to the table in the middle of the circle. Her earrings dangled, her heels clicked, and her silk scarf matched the green in her blouse: she couldn't have been further from the buttoned-up, conservative, tight-lipped clergywoman I'd been expecting.

I selected a mug covered in neon smiley faces and poured myself some tea. My hands were always looking for something to hold, a distraction to still their constant vibration. Janet sat down in a winged-back chair to my right, settling like a windup toy gone slack.

"Why don't we go around the circle and introduce ourselves, and maybe share what brought us here," she said.

I stared at her dumbly.

"I'm Lindsay," I said.

"Welcome," six tired voices, plus Janet's chipper one, replied.

The student sitting beside me seemed to understand that I wasn't ready to say what brought me in. So we said hello to Jessie, whose mother had died of a heart attack; Ben, whose girlfriend had died in a car crash; Paul, whose parents had both passed of cancer the summer before; Mya, whose father had been murdered in a faraway country; Annie, whose grandmother had slid into dementia before her grandfather shot himself in bed; and Kumar, who had lost his younger brother to a drunk driver.

"Eat cookies! Does everyone have tea? Has it been an okay week?" Janet asked.

We made halfhearted rustlings toward our cups, still too hot to drink from.

"It's hard to go through the motions when your mind is so far away," Jessie said.

Janet launched into a story. Her long-winded tales revolved around distant relatives, friends, and former students, and had less to do with religion than with faith. I was relieved that she didn't say anything about God working in mysterious ways, as so many had mumbled at my mother's funeral. Her hands orchestrated the air as she talked, silver bracelets glinting in the lamplight. Janet's goal was simply to make us feel better, if only by relating our pain to someone else's.

The sky turned from blue to bruised to black outside the window. We passed the tissue box to whoever needed it. We ate cookies at Janet's command, and for at least a few minutes of the two hours that I sat there, mostly silent, it did feel like all I needed was a baked good and a sympathetic ear.

I started going every Friday night, until I was able to say what had brought me there.

"Hi. I'm Lindsay, and my mom disappeared for six weeks."

"Hi, I'm Jessie, and my mom passed from a heart attack."

And around the circle we went.

Maybe Janet knew that her lengthy stories were the respite we needed from our own battered heads. My mind still raced with details about the missing person case. But in Janet's denlike office, it was one thing at a time. I could mention the barnacles stuck to my mother's submerged car and then allow the chaplain to carry me away on the tide of her kind voice.

Every week, she reminded us that grieving is a full-time job, one that we were cramming into a two-hour interval on Friday nights, between classes and work and everything else. I shared with strangers all the things I couldn't say to my father or brothers. I joked about wanting to set the four trash barrels on the Main Green on fire. Funeral pyres. We planned a one-year anniversary gathering in which we'd meet by the barrels at noontime on March 17 and douse them in kerosene. The flames would rise and I'd say how much easier this whole grieving thing would be if we weren't surrounded by constant reminders of our misfortune. But it was an idle fantasy, and the one-year anniversary of my mom's death passed uneventfully. I stayed holed up in my room. I knew I didn't have the guts to set school property ablaze, just as I knew that flaming barrels wouldn't change a thing. The metal probably wouldn't burn very well and then I'd have to walk by the charred remains every day. I had never hated inanimate objects before.

But we listened as everyone shared his own burning-barrels fantasy, and we didn't laugh or judge, because we understood, above all else, the futility of grieving, and how we had to do it anyway.

When crying no longer satisfied, we laughed. We had learned firsthand that there's nothing funny about death, but living through it is sometimes so absurd that we couldn't help but find humor in all the inconvenient ways that grief manifested itself. Sleeping through multiple alarm clocks, hallucinating after not sleeping for days on end, falling down the stairs, falling up the stairs, eating only apples, eating only pastries, crying at the bus stop, forgetting not only every answer but also your name on a final exam, bursting into tears because someone looked at you wrong, pulling a muscle by trying to literally outrun the pain. My new friends smiled when

I told them how certain I'd been that my anxiety attack was a heart attack. Plagued by strange ailments and injuries, we were all frequent visitors to the health center.

It became a running joke that at least one of my brothers and usually my dad would call during the meeting. I still wasn't answering my cell phone much, but it was during those meetings that I was able to see Brad's efforts as the best he could do, and more than I ever could have done. And Chris just wanted to know that I'd be okay. My brothers and I had never been big on saying "I love you," but this was what I felt, more than anything, when I heard them calling me every Friday night: a raw, unadulterated love coursing through my veins. I wanted us to make it through.

I rarely saw Janet or the other students around campus during the week, and yet there was a currency of emotion between us, a faith in each other if not in ourselves. Knowing that they'd all be there on Friday night got me through the rest of the week.

Dad was persistent with his phone calls, e-mails, and visits. He said things would never be this hard again. He said I just had to hold on. Despite my wariness in trusting a parent again, I was slowly coming around to the idea of my dad as support system. But no matter how many times Janet and the group told me that my mother's death wasn't my fault—despite the evidence I presented them of our New Year's Eve fight—I wasn't ready to forgive myself. And after all that Brad had reminded me of on Christmas, I couldn't stop searching for answers, the sense behind the suicide. I was hoping for a way to turn my mother's death back into an accident, which might make it somewhat easier to live with. And I knew there was only one place where I might find what I was looking for.

Chapter Ten

AS THE ONE-YEAR anniversary came and went, Granite Pier started creeping into my head more and more. I couldn't help but turn my mother's death into a beautifully tragic movie that looped through my mind:

Her white station wagon pulls onto the pier, headlights beaming into the darkness. A full moon hangs above a wooden dock that extends into the Atlantic, straight and narrow, one way, a road out. There's no one around for miles. The pier looks just like our old dock at the boatyard in Wickford.

Her right hand rests lazily on the gearshift, the same way she steered *Pippins,* her fingers loose on the tiller. Her open palm conveys an easy confidence, nothing to worry about, no need to rush. She's had a few glasses of Chardonnay and everything is soft around the edges. Humming along to the oldies station on the radio, she reapplies her mauve lipstick in the rearview mirror.

What happens next happens fast, keeping in character with her frequent mood swings. No second-guessing; only conviction. Her left foot releases the clutch while the right floors the gas pedal. Her fist pushes up through the gears: first to fifth, the motions second nature. She grips the wheel in her left hand, her ring finger without diamonds for the first time in years. Her eyes are fixed on the dock, bright and shining as it slides beneath the car. Her eyes are emerald in the moonlight.

The pier runs out of boards a half mile offshore. The car launches. The tires spin. The engine caterwauls. She sails toward the moon. The car plummets to the inky Atlantic, my mother buckled up, holding tight, prepared to ride out the storm. A captain never abandons ship.

The engine's whine gives way to a thunderous splash, followed by a cannonball, a whirlpool. Her eyes are wide open but she is not scared. She is not thinking about her three kids or her job or her new house in the mountains. All that is behind her now, back on solid ground. She is not thinking about anything other than the beauty of this moment: the water rising around the car, dark but for two white, shimmering beams emanating from her headlights.

And up above, the waves dissipate until the surface is calm again, betraying no sign of what just went under.

That's how I imagined it, anyway.

I was taking four classes and working a few nights a week at a basement eatery on campus, making pizza, smoothies, and falafel. I kept my baseball-capped head down while an endless line of hungry students placed orders. Strawberry breeze smoothie with a fat-burning booster. Falafel, no lettuce. Fried dough, the grease jumping out of the vat to burn my forearms. At one a.m., I walked the dark campus back to my dorm, where I'd scrub flour and blender spillage off my arms in the empty bathroom.

I picked up a second job monitoring a computer lab in the art building, more for needing somewhere to go than needing eight bucks an hour. I was afraid of spending too much time alone in my tiny dorm room. Cassidy managed the darkroom two flights below my new job, and I often left the lab open to go talk to her until the security guard came around to lock up at midnight.

She was slowly gaining weight, but her nails were still ridged and yellow, her spine still visible when she hunched over her biology homework. We talked about how much better things would be once we graduated. Nothing specific, just better all around. We needed a future bigger than dorm rooms cluttered with cans of lukewarm Ensure and old missing person flyers.

What I wanted was a way to coil up my emotions, one by one, like I'd always done with *Pippins*'s dock lines. When we weren't out sailing, I'd run from slip to slip along D Dock, crouching by rusty cleats to spiral the remaining few feet of bowline that trailed into the water or threatened to trip a careless walker. Halfway down the dock, a garden hose hung neatly on a hook, for boaters who needed to rinse the salt off their decks. When I was done with the lines, they matched the hose, coil for coil, a simple kind of order on a listless summer day. Every boat on the dock seemed a mystery afloat—what went on below deck I only glimpsed through egg-shaped cabin windows—and tidying up their bowlines was an excuse to peer in and imagine for a moment life aboard another vessel.

But everything kept tangling into knots: the wooden dock fantasy, the one-year anniversary, details from the forty days she was missing, the birthday fight, all of it. I knew that the only way I could possibly make sense of my mother's death was by going to Granite Pier.

My dad had cornered me on the morning of the memorial service, as though he could already see my plan forming.

"You can't go there. I know you think it'll help, but it won't," he said.

"Fine."

"Promise me you won't go."

"Okay."

I knew I'd made a promise I wouldn't be able to keep. Sooner or later I would go to Granite Pier. Only there would I learn what kind of sweetness had enticed my mother into the water. I had to feel the pier beneath my feet in order to understand what had made her drive off it. Maybe then I could even forgive her.

During the forty days she was missing, I hardly ever doubted that we'd find her alive. I understood where each clue could lead and chose to disbelieve any information that would support an unacceptable outcome. But the evidence of her car underwater had been incontrovertible. The detectives ruled out foul play and closed the case, leaving my mother's death adrift between suicide and accident. Their job was done; mine was just beginning. Granite Pier was the only place I hadn't searched. After resisting the temptation for a year, I got ready to go.

I met Cassidy for dinner right before leaving campus on a Friday night. We carried take-out containers from the dining hall to the deserted basement of the student center. Two flights above us, the bereavement group was probably still in session, but given the task ahead of me, I'd chosen to take a week off from Janet's stories.

"Are you sure you need to do this?" Cassidy asked.

An overhead television was tuned to CNN, the volume muted. The tables were scattered with wrappers and coffee cups. A reporter gestured to a war-torn country behind him. The camera panned over a pile of rubble.

I looked away and nodded.

"Then I won't tell you not to."

"I just have to see it."

"Do you want me to come?"

"I'll be back Sunday night, don't worry."

It started raining as soon as I got on the highway, heading north toward Beverly. I turned on the windshield wipers and listened to the dull thwack of the right blade for the next two hours. It had fallen off in a storm, and my dad had reattached it with wire.

Before I could go to the pier, I had to go to his house, that place he kept calling my home. I needed to see my father even as I was about to break the promise I'd made him.

Maggie kept me occupied on Saturday. Playing hide-and-seek with her, I could almost forget. Crouching in claw-footed bathtubs or third-floor closets, letting her find me was almost enough. I wanted to be talked out of the next day's journey, wanted Maggie's seven-year-old spirit to carry me above a misery she knew nothing about.

Dad kept saying how nice it was to have me around. A year had passed but we didn't talk about it. Sunday morning he served Maggie and me breakfast in bed. Every time I visited he would make cinnamon raisin bread from scratch and carry it up on a tray at seven thirty, complete with coffee and fruit. Maggie would jump into bed with me and sip her hot chocolate. I couldn't remember my dad ever doing this before my mom died.

I slid one hand around my coffee mug and eyed the toast. Dad was hovering just outside my bedroom door, waiting for me to take a bite.

"I have to go back to school after breakfast," I said.

"Stay the night, head back early tomorrow."

"I can't, I've got work to do."

He sighed, knowing he couldn't change my mind or break me of the stubbornness I'd inherited from my mom. I brought the empty tray downstairs a few minutes later. Dad sat down on the black wooden chair in the corner. No one sat in that chair other than him, and he sat there only twice a day: once in the morning to tie up his work boots, and again at night, pulling them off. Before Maggie had gotten too big for it, he'd pick her up on his knees and chant the same tune he'd sung to me so many years before:

Choo-choo to Boston
Choo-choo to Lynn
Watch out Maggie
Or you'll fall in!

At the last line he'd split his knees apart and pretend to drop her as she shrieked and clung to his shoulders.

He double-knotted his laces, zipped his hooded sweatshirt, and walked out to the garage. Ever since retiring from his corporate job seven years earlier, he'd been dressing like a carpenter.

I packed up my things and hugged Maggie good-bye, telling her not to cry, knowing she would anyway, for a few minutes, and then she'd be okay. I carried my backpack to the garage and found my dad doing what he always did before I left: putting air in the tires and checking the oil. When he finished he leaned against the hood. His hands were greasy, his wiry hair peppered with more white strands than gray. He was fifty-five and it occurred to me that he could no longer pass for a handsome forty. We all seemed to be aging fast lately; every few weeks I found another gray strand in my hairline that I preferred to think of as silver.

"I love you, Linds," he said.

He had that faraway look like he wanted to say more. But it wasn't a convenient time to resume the conversation we'd been having off and on for a few months, the one in which he said he was worried about me and never meant for things to get so messed up. I opened the driver's-side door, stepped in, and started the engine. If we had that discussion I knew I wouldn't make it to the pier. Rockport was only fourteen miles up the coast from his house.

He motioned for me to roll down the window.

"Drive safe," he said, his blue eyes wet and shining.

I held my gaze on the garage, so cluttered with his tools that a car couldn't even fit. He reached in and squeezed my shoulder.

"See you soon," I said.

Getting out of the driveway was sometimes the hardest part. I adjusted the rearview mirror while I waited for a break in the stream of cars coming around the corner. Dad was still standing in front of the garage, hands in pockets, watching me go.

Just knowing that he was open to such conversations was enough of a change from the stone-faced silence that had lasted for months after my mom's death. Or maybe it was just that I could finally hear what he'd been saying all along.

I turned on the radio in hopes of distraction, but every song was wrong. The classic rock station was too familiar, rap too angry, and pop too annoying. The buttons on the dashboard tended to overheat, as if the whole electrical system were about to melt. I skipped through the stations with my index finger burning.

I hated lying. But if I'd told my dad where I was really going, he would have taken my keys away and driven me back to school in his truck. Ever since my brief stay in the Maine hospital, my grieving methods were not to be trusted. Staying away from Granite Pier was the only thing he'd asked of me all year.

I drove slowly, wishing Rockport were farther away. I wanted to drive all day and all night, wanted those fourteen miles to be fourteen hundred. But the miles quickly slid by.

My dad was my dad: loving him was a given. But with my mother's dislike of him constantly vented to me over the years, I took on her feelings as my own. After twelve months without her, I was finally starting to see my father through my own eyes, and I was startled to discover how much I genuinely *liked* him. His strange sense of humor, his preference for shabby clothes, his dogged persistence in trying to make things better. And not just the forty-room house, either. I'd always known he could do anything with his hands, but it was his heart whose capacity I was beginning to see. He'd always wanted to be there for Chris, Brad, and me—he'd just never had much of a chance until I was twenty and the boys a few years older. I wanted to believe that it was never too late to start over, but my mother had convinced herself otherwise, and it bothered me to know how similar our temperaments were.

By this point I had only a few miles to go. Rockport wasn't so different from Newburyport, where my mom had lived thirty miles up the coast. They were both fishing towns-turned-tourist traps, both wealthy Massachusetts suburbs clinging to an old notion of New England charm. Colorful buoys festooned the sides of houses and well-worn lobster pots doubled as garden accessories. Tourists would start swarming in another few months, but in the meantime, the roads along the harbor seemed little more than an empty stage set with seafood shacks and gift shops. I felt sick as soon as I saw the water.

I pulled over to consult the Google directions I'd printed that morning. Losing my way felt like one last chance to turn back. What I didn't yet know was that Brad had gone to the pier the night after our mother was found, meeting with the harbormaster and examining photographs of her car being pulled out of the water. I drove to the pier under the impression that neither of my brothers had ever been there.

I kept the water on my right as I passed a few forlorn-looking shops and restaurants. My directions led me out of town and up a hill that extended above the harbor. I checked my map and made a hard right onto Wharf Road. The houses fell away and the bay opened below me.

I drove slowly downhill, waiting for the road to become a straight and narrow pier, built of wood and nails, pilings and planks. A launchpad into the Atlantic. The hill led to a pier so unlike the one I had envisioned that I checked my map again, thinking I must have made a wrong turn. But this was Granite Pier.

It was more of a dirt road slapped atop a peninsula of boulders. A promontory rather than a dock. Snowman-sized rocks lined the end of the pier a quarter mile out, spaced every five feet or so, presumably to prevent vehicles from going over the edge.

I parked in the middle of the pier, nervous about driving too close to the end. As I walked to the boulders for a better view, I could think only of how Granite Pier was supposed to look: the dock that would be just wide enough for her car to launch from, the dock that would take us back to our past.

Rockport was tucked off to the right, the pier serving as a breakwall to protect the harbor from high seas. I stood at the edge and looked down. Rocks bigger than tombstones extended a hundred feet in front of me, from pier to water, creating a mild slope rather than the sudden drop-off I had envisioned. Waves slapped against granite slabs far below. It seemed impossible that a car—a low-to-the-ground Subaru, no less—could drive across all those craggy boulders. But I also couldn't imagine her car launching across at least a hundred feet of sky.

I walked the edge of the pier, one foot in front of the other, heel to sneakered toe. I counted my footsteps between each boulder, trying to determine whether any of the openings along the perimeter were wide enough for her Outback to slip through. By my calculations, the gap slightly left of the pier's center was maybe large enough, but only if she'd precisely calculated the angle. And if that angle required such precision, how could she also get the running start—racing downhill on Wharf Road and holding fast on the gas pedal as she crossed the pier—that might make it possible to clear the boulders? And how could she be that precise if she'd been drinking, as I suspected she had?

I climbed onto the rocks that sloped out over the front edge of the pier. The smell of seaweed clogged the air. I leaped from boulder to boulder, careful not to catch my feet in any of the dark crevices in between. I'd soon be close enough to the water to feel the spray of the breaking waves. But it was March, and the water couldn't have been more than fifty degrees, and I was already freezing in my thin jacket. I looked up at the pier behind me, jutting out from the land like an amputated limb. I'd been wrong to break my promise and come here. I was no detective. I was nothing more or less than my mother's daughter, and I was still searching for her.

I had wanted her final dive to be like a game my brothers and I played when we were little, lining up on the shore of the beach, barreling our scrawny chests and bending our scraped knees. When each wave pulled back toward the ocean, a little more sand slid out from under our heels. The earth beneath us pulled away. It didn't matter who fell first, because we were already running into the waves, never looking back to worry over our footprints, the traces of which were already disappearing.

I crouched down on a rock, wrapped my arms around my knees, and watched it all come up: *Pippins* gliding under Jamestown Bridge. Mom diving off the boom, breaststroking away from the hull, surfacing to spit and say, "Whew! Beautiful." Dad stenciling the lettering on the stern of the dinghy he'd just built for the boys and me, *Chuckles* in wet green paint. The time the basement flooded on Christmas Eve while Mom wept by the busted sump pump, saying, "I can't fix this," while Brad scooped buckets up the stairs and Chris and I paddled around in an inflatable canoe. How we laughed about it the next morning as we tore open our gifts.

I was wrong to assume that her suicide was a relatively straightforward matter that I'd understand and be able to put behind me if I went to the place where it had happened. Seeing those boulders and the craggy drop-off they created, I was more confused than ever. But even though driving off Granite Pier would require a near impossible amount of precision and velocity, I still chose to believe that my mother had achieved just that. I would never admit it aloud, but I was clinging to the belief that there was something heroic, or at least brave, about committing suicide.

But forget the pier for a minute. Look to the harbor now. Nothing ambiguous about the role *it* played. Water always finds its way in, filling spaces with the shapes we give it. Her lips, her lungs, a leak in the hull. The Atlantic everywhere, surging and swelling, the moment of euphoria as oxygen failed to find her brain, and then giddy, high before the blackout. That much I could be certain of.

I tucked low on the rocks, bracing myself against the wind, wishing I could take back our final argument, wishing more than anything that I could have saved her. And then all at once, shivering in the damp breeze, I could no longer make excuses for my mother. I would never know exactly how or why she had drowned herself. And for the first time, I understood that it wasn't about me. Committing suicide was bigger than an argument, bigger than empty-nest syndrome or isolation or fear of starting over, bigger than anything I knew about the one person I thought I knew best.

The ocean looked ugly for the first time in my life, a lethal dose of blue. Rockport was a meaningless tourist trap we had occasionally passed through, devoid of any personal relevance I could grasp. Maybe that's what hurt the most: as I stood on the boulders, my mother became completely unknowable to me. I couldn't fathom the hell she must have been going through to think that the only way out was underwater.

I scrambled up the rocks, reaching the top of the pier and getting back in my car. I was rubbing my hands in front of the heater when I looked up and saw an ambulance parked a hundred yards from me. The only other vehicle in sight, it faced away from the harbor toward the open sea, where the waves flatlined into a blue horizon.

I looked over as I passed the ambulance on my way back to solid ground. The driver's face was shielded behind a newspaper. He was most likely on his lunch break, lost in the sports pages and a sandwich. Had it become necessary, though, I knew that this stranger would have turned on his sirens and saved me. And I thought maybe this was my mom looking out for me even as she let me down.

I sped out of Rockport and followed the signs toward I-95 South, eager to put Massachusetts behind me. The highway had become a wind tunnel, gusts barreling out of the trees on either side. It felt as though my little Jeep might get blown three lanes sideways, lifted and flipped into a ditch. Sometimes when that breeze picked up or I hit a turn too fast, I thought maybe it wouldn't be so bad to throttle the gas and let the wind take me. Just close my eyes and feel the ground beneath me give. At least it would look like an accident.

What I wanted more than anything was to have my mom riding beside me in the passenger seat, rolling down the windows and singing along with Paul, her favorite Beatle. It wouldn't even matter where we were going, because we would be together and none of this would have happened.

"Little darling, it's been a long cold lonely winter—"

But somehow I always managed to slow down and keep on going.

———————

For a long time I would continue to believe that my mom had, despite the odds, somehow cleared all those boulders and hurtled toward Rockport Harbor far below. It would take me a while to accept a much more likely story of what had happened on the pier.

Reading her autopsy report was what changed my understanding. In addition to describing almost all of my mother's organs as *largely unremarkable,* the report revealed how little external damage there had been to her body. The only cut was a *small laceration of the medial right ankle about 1" in length with some adjacent purple bruising.* Her car, I remembered, had been lifted ashore with almost no visible damage other than a sandy interior and one broken windshield. The action movie version I'd so long believed in—with all those rocks to clear and all that distance to plummet—suddenly became impossible. A death like that would involve a lot more wreckage than a one-inch laceration and a broken windshield.

Granite Pier materialized before my eyes as I read the toxicology report: *none detected* for methanol, isopropanol, benzodiazepines, cocaine, fentanyl, methadone, opiates, and oxycodone. And then *0.04% ethanol,* the one fact from the report I'd known all along, as Brad had told me. I'd yearned to find some shred of comfort in learning that our mother had been drunk when she drove off the pier, but a blood alcohol level of 0.04 percent amounted to the same two glasses of wine she'd consumed every night with dinner. Despite the facts, I had chosen to believe she'd been completely intoxicated. I reasoned that the amount of ethanol found in her system was relatively low because her body had likely been decomposing for weeks underwater, providing plenty of time to dissipate higher alcohol contents into the Atlantic. I'd never bothered to see if there was any science behind this theory.

But seeing *0.04% ethanol* right there on the report, I finally understood a hard truth: my mom had consumed a couple of glasses of wine, nothing more. She was under the influence, but by no means intoxicated. More than likely she was functioning at her normal level of lucidity when she stepped on the gas pedal.

I felt as if I were standing back on Granite Pier, only this time I was looking not at the boulders and the water but off to my right, where the rocks bottomed out and the harbor curved around toward Rockport. Looking at a boat-launching ramp. I must have seen it when I went to the pier, but I'd been so preoccupied with the boulders that I managed to completely dismiss the ramp. Reading the autopsy, suddenly it seemed more likely that my mom had driven down the ramp and floated out a ways before sinking. A gentler drowning: a way for her body to come up mostly intact, even as the water flooded her lungs.

Launching ramps like the one at Granite Pier had been as much a part of my childhood as *Pippins*'s old dock in Wickford. Growing up we owned a small Boston Whaler named *Mystery Girl*. Whenever we couldn't make the two-hour drive down to Wickford, we'd trailer *Mystery Girl* to the nearest coastal town and back her down a ramp into the water. Easing her out until she floated, we would unhook the trailer, park the car, grab a cooler, and head out on the water for the day.

One of the only photographs I have of my mother taken in the last few years of her life shows her standing in the teal blue interior of our Whaler. She's alone in the boat and it's not clear whether the person taking the picture (was it me?) is standing onshore or on another boat. Eight sailboats are frozen in the background. She's most likely out watching a regatta; maybe Uncle George is racing and she's cheering on her brother. She wears jeans, a Windbreaker, and a red baseball cap. It doesn't appear to be summer anymore. She's smiling, but her mouth is closed; you couldn't call it a grin. Her eyes are hidden behind her Ray-Bans. She has one hand in her pocket and the other on the steering wheel, as if she's about ready to go. *Mystery Girl* is written in dark Gothic script running the length of the hull.

I believed in the launching ramp version of her death for all of twenty-four hours. Something about it still wasn't adding up, though. Her car had been found off the end of the pier, not the end of the ramp. A car was too heavy for even a few weeks of changing tides to carry it from the ramp out to the end of the pier, a distance of at least a quarter mile. And so I summoned some courage, looked up the number, and reached for my phone. I dialed the one man I thought might have the answer I was seeking, a man who knew Granite Pier better than anyone else: the Rockport harbormaster.

Making this phone call had always seemed like a bad idea. For so long I'd avoided any evidence that might alter my understanding of how my mother had died—just as during the forty days she was missing, I had dismissed any clues that didn't fit with my choice theories. But it was time to get my facts straight.

After I explained who I was, the harbormaster put me on speakerphone. There were two harbormasters, as it turned out—one male, one female—and both of them had witnessed my mother's car being pulled out of the harbor. My voice faltered when I said I was hoping to ask them some questions, but I pressed on.

"Based on where her car was found and since there wasn't much damage, do you think she drove off the pier or the boat-launching ramp? I'm just trying to figure out the most likely point of entry. I know this must seem strange to be calling you a few years after—"

I forced myself to stop talking and wait for a response, no matter what it might change or confirm.

"The fishing pier," he said.

"Yeah, that seems like the only way," she added.

"But how would she clear all those boulders without damaging her car?" I asked.

"There are no boulders off the fishing pier," she said. "It's *below* the rocks."

"Of course we'll never know, but that's where her car was found, and that'd be the easiest place to drive off," he added.

"I didn't know there was a lower level on the pier," I said.

"Where the fishing boats unload their catch, that makes the most sense."

I hung up the phone and got on the Internet. I felt faint as I clicked on Google maps. I'd never allowed myself to search online for Granite Pier before, let alone in satellite view. But it was loading, coming in clearer, and there it was: *the fishing pier.*

A paved road ran parallel to the promontory I'd parked on, but much lower and flatter, almost at sea level. Below the boulders. A turnoff on Wharf Road led down there, but on my visit I'd either overlooked the lower pier or I'd blocked it from my memory in favor of a more dramatic plummet. But from the fork in Wharf Road a driver would have at least a quarter mile to accelerate. She could do it at night when no one was around. There wouldn't be a huge drop-off or all those boulders to contend with, and the water wouldn't be too shallow to submerge in, as it might have been over by the launching ramp.

Her autopsy: the lack of cuts and bruising.

The fishing pier: a clean entry, a quick plunge.

The puzzle pieces suddenly fit together. Like the harbormaster said, *that seems like the only way.*

The Google map and the sudden recognition of where my mother must have launched from didn't tell me when she had died or why. There was no lightbulb, no aha! moment, no epiphany. I still wouldn't know what to make of the sightings in northern Maine. I still wouldn't know whether my mother had drowned that first night or if it was later on that she went under, while we were searching for her and she couldn't bear the thought of coming home. I would never know what my mother was thinking in the moment before she stepped on the gas pedal. A map couldn't tell me these things. A map couldn't tell me why. *Of course we'll never know.*

But the map did matter. The map rearranged my memory: her death hadn't been the brave hurtling dive I'd so long imagined. It was a softer launch, followed by a few seconds or minutes of floating, until the water took her under, until the water found its way into her lungs. Hers was a smaller shipwreck, not off the part of the pier where tourists went to admire the view and locals went to walk their dogs, but lower down, where those who made their living off the sea hauled up their catch. Whether this was an easier version to accept was beside the point. After years of thinking about little else, I wanted, finally, to stop imagining my mother's death.

I would not go back to Granite Pier. Once had been too much, even though I'd stood on the wrong part of the pier with the wrong scenario in mind. I was almost grateful that my dramatic imaginings had for so long buffered me from reading the map as it really was. Thinking I'd figured out my Mystery Girl and getting her wrong most of the time struck me as a more realistic way to go about things. I was slowly learning how to live in a space of unanswerable questions, where the only peace to be found was in letting go of the questions themselves.

I remember how carefully my mother zipped *Pippins*'s nautical charts in plastic sleeves and stowed them below deck after mapping out our course. I remember how rubbery the sleeves felt and how blue the paper ocean was. We lost the charts somewhere. After all this time they'd be so sun faded or waterlogged that they wouldn't help me to find her anyway. This was memory. This was the ocean. Nothing was airtight and nothing stayed dry for very long.

Chapter Eleven

Back at school, time crawled past just as slowly. By senior year I had moved to an apartment off-campus, where I shared a kitchen with a bunch of ice hockey players. Cassidy's place was only a few blocks away and we cooked dinner together more often than not, fantasizing about where we'd go after Providence. She was looking into farmwork in Montana, while I had New York on my mind. Over warm bowls of kale and brown rice, we talked of the future as if it were a door flung wide. *Away* was where we wanted to go. Passing a pint of Ben & Jerry's back and forth for dessert, we indulged in imagining ourselves elsewhere.

In addition to the bereavement group, I started spending an hour a week on a therapist's couch. When I complained of going through the meaningless motions of class and work, she said this "holding pattern" was exactly what I needed, as if I were an airplane awaiting permission to land. I fixed my eyes on graduation as some kind of landing, after which real life could begin. Beyond wanting it to be free of calamity, I had no idea what this "real life" would look like.

When this same therapist called my mind a *black hole,* I started seeing someone off-campus instead, a woman with fancy shoes who slowly cracked my brittle façade. We made lists of things I wanted to say to my brothers and my father. Lists of things I should and shouldn't do, tallying all the ways to keep living on yellow lined pads of paper. And week by week, we started checking them off.

I made myself answer the phone whenever my brothers or my dad called, and I tried to call them every now and then too. It didn't matter that there were long stretches of silence sometimes. We were trying.

Whenever I felt the need to get away from Providence, I drove a half hour south to my uncle George's house in Wickford. He lived across the street from the boatyard where I'd spent all those immortal summers. His doors were never locked, and I often showed up unannounced. If George was still at work, I'd help myself to some wine and ease into the hot tub on his back deck.

If I stood up in the water, I could see the parking lot behind the work shed where *Pippins* had been dry-docked for years. But *Pippins* wasn't there anymore. A few months after Mom's memorial service, the manager of the boatyard had called to say we could no longer store the boat there. My brothers wanted to sell it, and so one morning Chris drove down to Providence and picked me up, and together we went to see what had become of our old wooden boat. We hadn't been to Wickford in a few years, but the route was more familiar than anything else we'd felt in a while.

The boatyard was deserted. We parked in the empty lot and

walked behind the maintenance shed that we'd circled so many times on our bikes a decade earlier. My eyes scanned the bellies of the dry-docked boats, looking for the kelly green underside of *Pippins*. Dismantled masts were stacked along the side of the shed, and the sailboats looked out of place on their metal stands. After wandering through the maze for a few minutes, I spied *Pippins* in the back of the lot. Chris dragged a ladder over, leaned it against the hull, and climbed aboard. I hoisted myself up under the railing, careful not to kick over the ladder. The cockpit was full of brittle leaves. I sat in Mom's spot, my hand draped over the tiller and my feet propped up. The cushions were gone, the wooden benches warped and water stained. My hands were freezing, my thumbs all hacked up again. I never even gave them time to heal before I peeled the scabs wide open.

The cabin was locked. I peered through the small oval windows to where I once slept. Chris crouched over the translucent fiberglass hatch above his old sleeping quarters. There were no cushions on the bunks. No sleeping bags, no atlases, no floorboards. A milk jug floated in a puddle of dirty brown bilge water. The interior had been stripped, and *Pippins*'s ribs jutted out, splintered and sodden. I crawled back to the ladder and descended. I didn't know how we had let things get so bad.

We walked past the travel lift and down to the dinghy dock. Lately Dad had been asking about *Chuckles*, the rowboat he'd built years ago and now wanted back so that he could teach Maggie how to sail. I wasn't sure what had become of *Chuckles*, though.

There were hardly any boats in the water. The surface was crusted over with a thin veneer of ice. And then I saw it: *Chuckles*, half sunk in the shallow water. We had forgotten to take it out of the harbor, and now it was on its way under. A small shipwreck of neglect. I could not tell my father what I'd found.

There was no excuse for letting *Chuckles* sink and letting *Pippins* rot. If anything, my mother had waited until she knew my brothers and I could take care of ourselves before going under herself. She took care of us in the best way she knew how, which was more than I could say for myself as I stood on the dinghy dock looking at what had become of the boat my father had built for his children. *Chuckles*. There had been plans to build a sister dinghy, plans to name it *Giggles,* plans to race them across Stevens Pond. But following through on plans had never been our strong suit.

As it turned out, *Pippins* would at least not end up as scrap wood. George managed to find a friend of a friend who agreed to take the boat for free. He was a wooden boat enthusiast who undertook the massive project of gutting the cabin, refurbishing the keel, repainting the hull, and trying to make her sing again. I never met the man who was giving a new life to our old boat, but hearing about him made me happy, and I just hoped he wouldn't change her name.

With *Pippins* gone, our old storage spot had been taken by another boat. Its owner had anticipated the off-season more than we ever had, shrink-wrapping the hull like a giant Thanksgiving turkey, shielding it from the rain and snow. Seeing this other boat all snug in its wrapping only reminded me of how unprepared we'd been for the storm.

My brothers and I no longer had reason to talk on the phone five times a day. Now we called just to check in. Our faux-casual conversations hurt more than acknowledging all that we had lost, but it was a start, and I knew we'd go to any lengths for one another. First we had to put some space between us, though.

Following his college graduation, Brad hitched a trailer to his truck and moved to Portland, Oregon, where he'd landed a job as an environmental consultant. Of all the mementoes to take with him, he chose the biggest: a broken-in brown leather couch, chair, and love seat from the living room of our ski condo. So many nights we'd fallen asleep sprawled on those couches after a day on the slopes and a bowl of our mom's homemade chili.

Chris had wanted to keep the condo, insisting that it was full of happy memories with our mom and could be the site of more ski trips with our own future families. But Brad and I wanted to sell. Remembering vacations was too taxing. Majority ruled and we sold the condo while the yellow house was still on the market.

In Portland, Brad set up the couches in the house he'd be sharing with his girlfriend. Whenever he called, I imagined him sitting on our old couches in his new living room. He said he liked it out west, which I feared meant he was never coming back. Brad was studying to obtain his pilot's license, and whenever I called Dad, he was usually on the other line with my brother, discussing airplanes and FAA regulations and how to respond to every conceivable problem a pilot might encounter while flying.

Meanwhile, I was trying to untangle my own problems with the well-dressed therapist. I was still going about trying to feel better in questionable ways, and there was one thing I'd done that I couldn't bring myself to tell her about.

I was spending a weekend at my dad's when I found myself up on the third floor, rifling through storage boxes, as I did every time

I was there. In one of the boxes I came across my mother's jewelry: several gold necklaces, pendants, bracelets, and rings that I hadn't seen since packing her apartment a year earlier.

Next thing I knew, I had tossed it all in a plastic bag and gone out to my car. Forty-five minutes later I parked outside what appeared to be a shabby house in Salem, New Hampshire. The building had always caught my eye because it seemed so out of place on the side of the three-lane road, its clapboard siding and faded shingled roof suspect among so many car dealerships and strip malls. A neon sign flashed in the upstairs window: CASH FOR GOLD.

I put the bag in my purse and locked the doors before crossing the parking lot to the Cash for Gold building. I looked up as the door slammed shut behind me, my pupils dilating in the dark lobby. A security camera surveyed me from the top of a staircase.

One flight up, I came to a deserted lobby. A dusty plant sat forgotten in the corner. My mom would have been able to identify it by genus and species, but her knowledge of flora hadn't rubbed off on me and all I knew was that it looked close to death.

A large bulletproof window separated the lobby from an office. It reminded me of the entryway of the Newburyport police station, where we'd gone to report our mother missing.

A man appeared on the other side of the barrier, looking bored.

"Can I help you?" he said through a cutout in the glass.

"I brought some jewelry to sell. How does this work?"

"You give it, we weigh it, cash determined by weight."

"What do you do with it?"

"We melt it."

"Melt it?"

"Yeah, melt it then sell it to manufacturers to make new stuff."

"Oh."

I pulled the bag out of my purse and held it up to the window. The necklaces were tangled.

"Feed 'em through one by one."

I started with a gold chain, snaking it into the metal tray below the window. He dropped it onto a scale resting on the window ledge. I held my eyes on the scale and kept pushing necklaces under the window.

The man paused on his third trip to the scale. "Are you sure this is all yours to sell?"

"It's mine."

I could tell he was waiting for the story of how I came to have all these gold necklaces and bracelets at twenty years old, but I was tired of curious strangers. I didn't really know what had motivated me to sell some of my mom's jewelry. My mother simply had a lot of *stuff*. She saved half-melted candles just in case the power went out and she could coax old candlewicks back to flame. It's not like I was going to sell her big diamond ring or the turquoise pieces that I would wear. I was just trying to get rid of some of the clutter. I thought it might make me feel better; thought this was what people did when they had a mess to clean up. Figured I might as well try to make a little money off it.

I emptied a fistful of rings into the metal tray under the window, trying to act like I did this all the time.

He pushed the rings back through the slot. "I don't do diamonds. Take 'em to Boston, some shops around Chinatown will give you a good price for the stones."

"You won't take diamonds?"

He pointed to the neon sign flickering in the window behind him: CASH FOR GOLD. Visible to passersby on the road, the words were reversed from where I was standing.

I put the rings back in my purse and waited as he pulled a calculator and a legal pad from his desk drawer and began punching numbers and scribbling out a receipt. I'd brought only the rings that didn't have a story behind them—the ones my mother never wore, the small ones that barely fit on my pinkie. A stack of bills appeared, shuffled from one hand to the other as he counted. It looked like Monopoly money, so crisp and creaseless. He slid the bills into an envelope and pushed it through the slot. I took the stairs down two at a time.

I walked quickly to my car, certain that I was being watched. I braced myself for the outside world to confirm the guilt that was swarming my insides: sirens, handcuffs, my car getting struck by a freak lightning storm—whatever the punishment was, I hoped it would come quick.

At least I hadn't sold her rings. Only because the place wouldn't take diamonds, but still. I vowed to return them to her jewelry box the minute I got back to my dad's house.

The bulk of the envelope smacked of sacrilege, but I also had a feeling I'd been ripped off. Only when I reached the first stoplight did I count the bills. Mostly twenties, a couple of fifties. Gold to cash. Eight hundred dollars lay in my lap, while a fistful of my mom's jewelry was on its way to the smelter's pot. But not her best jewelry, I reassured myself. I told myself that it was just more housecleaning, but for a long time I would feel like I'd sold off a small part of my mother for a measly eight hundred bucks, and I wasn't even sure why.

Chris also was handling this whole business of "moving forward" much better than I was. He had bought a house in New Hampshire with his fiancée, Elizabeth, and they were planning a September wedding. In addition to my bridesmaid duties, Chris had asked me to prepare a brief speech acknowledging our mom. The wedding was fast approaching and I dreaded the very thought of standing at a podium to speak of the glaring absence in the pews.

The morning of the wedding I awoke feeling as if I was holding my breath. It'd been the same way at Brad's college graduation. Celebrating milestones felt all wrong without Mom there to shoot endless rolls of photographs; smiling and posing so soon after her death felt like betrayal. How could Chris be getting married sixteen months after she had died? He was doing what was best for him, but I had a hard time understanding how any kind of new bond could be made after all our mother had broken. It hadn't been my graduation and it wasn't my wedding to mope about, though. Besides, if Mom were there, she'd be smiling too.

I stood in my coppery satin dress and looked at my brothers, Chris facing his future wife in the front of the church, and Brad right behind him, his best man. I'd never seen them in tuxedos before.

It was the first time I'd given a speech since my mom's eulogy, to largely the same crowd of family and friends. I was just as nervous as I'd been a year and a half earlier, standing in my dad's living room. I smoothed the printout of my speech, which the priest had left tucked beneath a Bible on the podium.

My mom always knew that Chris and Elizabeth would get married someday. Since their sophomore year at the University of New Hampshire, my mom had their photo framed on her bedside table. In the picture, the happy couple stands in front of their dorm, Chris smiling in a baseball cap, and Liz grinning in a T-shirt. Today, they are more dressed up for their photo opportunity, but the sentiment is the same. Like a well-preserved photograph, their love has stood the test of time, and we honor them today.

I paused and looked up, locking eyes with Chris, seeking his approval.

Now we carry our mother's photograph with us in our hearts, comforted by the knowledge that she saw Chris and Elizabeth's relationship grow from a small seed into a tall tree. Chris, Brad, and I would just like to say thank you, Mom, for raising us to value love above all else. Thank you for showing us how to always be there for one another. You taught us the true meaning of family—unconditional love.

I glanced up again. Chris's eyes were shining and Brad's head was bowed. I plowed on, knowing that if I didn't start speaking again, my mascara would be running in a few seconds.

Today our family stands with open arms. I know you'd be so proud of your son Chris right now. You raised him right. Instilled with the values of trust, loyalty, and a good heart, Chris has everything he needs to start a wonderful life with Elizabeth. Thank you, Mom.

I made my way back to the line of bridesmaids. Someone else took the podium to read a passage from the Bible, but until the priest said, "I now pronounce you husband and wife," I couldn't hear anything other than the beating of my own noisy heart.

After the ceremony we mingled outside the church in the fading autumn sunlight. Dad came over and gave me a hug.

"You were great up there," he said.

"Thanks."

"I was worried you might be kind of negative."

"Why would I be negative?"

"This hasn't been easy on you."

I knew he wasn't talking about the wedding, just as I knew he couldn't say, "Losing your mom hasn't been easy on you." He was relieved that I was becoming more open to the idea of a future, not simply because I had to be, but also because that's what my mom would have wanted for me. Life was different without her, but it was still life, rearranged. I was glad my dad was becoming a central part of it. Yes, I still made poor choices—drinking too much, selling her jewelry, isolating myself—but in the scheme of things, I wasn't doing too badly. It's not like I'd dropped out of school and started shooting heroin. Even though I'd be the last to admit it, the pain of her absence was slowly moving from a stab wound to a deep bruise. Chris had just gotten married. Brad was learning to fly. I could live with some bruising.

"I'm proud of you, Linds," Dad said.

I winced whenever he said that. I wasn't out to make him proud, or so I claimed. But even as I'd promised myself that I wouldn't get close to him after everything that had happened, I couldn't help it. We were talking on the phone almost every day by my senior year.

He'd ask about school and I'd ask how his home improvements were coming along. We talked about our daily lives rather than dwelling on the forty days that had rearranged them.

From the church we drove to the reception hall, where we posed for pictures by a golf course and went inside to the dining room. I headed straight for the open bar and drank a vodka-cranberry a little too quickly. Dad had nothing stronger than Diet Coke all night. After the new bride danced with her father, Chris led me to the stage for the mother-groom number. I hadn't wanted to stand in for our mom, but I couldn't say no. The DJ put on James Taylor's "You've Got a Friend." Chris was practically holding me up as we swirled around the floor.

We spun past Dad, Michele, and Maggie, the flower girl falling asleep in her mother's lap. I saw Brad looking on, easily identifiable as the only one wearing a T-shirt. He'd loosened his tie, tossed off his tuxedo jacket, and unbuttoned his white shirt in the midst of his toast to the bride and groom. He read aloud from his T-shirt, which listed ten reasons why fishing is better than marriage:

1. If you hook a big one, feel free to go back for a second.
2. If you don't like what you catch, you can throw her back. . . .

Because they were brothers, his toast was perfectly inappropriate and everyone was laughing by the time he was halfway through the list.

Aunts and uncles and cousins blurred as we spun around the room. James Taylor was singing about how he'd be there, winter spring summer or fall. *Lord, I'll be there, yes I will.* How many times we'd sung along to this song as we drove to the mountains or the ocean, New Hampshire or Rhode Island. Chris was beaming at everyone as we circled the room. My feet were sore and I was getting sloppy.

"Keep it together," he whispered in my ear.

I got my two left feet back in line and danced with all the grace I could muster, because my brother was in love and all we had to do was call out her name, and even if she wasn't here, we were, and life spun on, for better or worse.

Chapter Twelve

CHRIS WOKE ME up at five forty-five and I stumbled out to his car half asleep. I'd been dreading this day for months. It was March again, 2008 this time: exactly two years had passed since our mother's death. My graduation was coming up in two months, but before I could receive a diploma and permission to leave Providence, there was this one task left for me to complete.

We were on our way to throw out the contents of our mother's house in North Conway. Our Realtor was showing the house and the basement was still full of boxes. If we wanted to sell the place, we had to empty it. I had assumed that Brad would be there to help, but it was a long flight from Portland and he was too busy with work to make the trip back for only the weekend.

We stopped at Dunkin' Donuts in the gray morning light. There was no need to talk this early except to order coffee. Like so much of what we'd been through, we saw little point in discussing the unpleasant task ahead. Chris turned on the CD player and James Taylor started singing our mom's favorite songs.

The sun came up and Dad called my cell phone. He knew about our weekend plans and had offered to help, but I had a feeling Mom would have wanted only my brothers and me digging through her stuff. Although she was gone, I still wanted to stay on her good side. So I asked him about his renovations instead.

"I just found a fireplace behind the bookshelf in Brad's room," he said.

I pictured my father running his hands over bricks that had gone untouched for decades.

"And Maggie helped me paint the walls. Light green."

This too I could picture, my dad and my little sister, running rollers up a wall, playing "guess the animal" while flecks of green paint splattered their hair. My father found his peace in building doors, sanding floors, and painting walls. Preserving what he could, making it as good as new. While he would keep working one room at a time, my brothers and I would empty and sell our mother's house. Whatever it took to move forward.

"Reception's bad here. I should go," I said.

"Okay, call me if you need anything. I love you, Linds."

"Love you too."

I would keep moving from one apartment to the next, but I was grateful that I had a home to return to, even if there would be sawhorses in the living room for years to come. There would always be a capable handyman around for whatever situation arose. And for the things my father couldn't fix, time would. It took me two years, but I was finally beginning to see what I could live with, and what I had to let go of.

Outside North Conway we stopped to rent a U-Haul. I got behind the wheel of the Explorer, and Chris followed in a big orange truck. We passed through town and turned into the steep driveway of the vacant house. The snow was still a few feet deep. The driveway had been hastily plowed and was slicked with ice. Mount Washington was barely visible through the low-lying clouds.

The task of maintaining the house had fallen to Chris and Elizabeth, who lived the closest. But their own house was still two hours south of North Conway, and driving up to cut the grass or fix a broken furnace on weekends could not have been easy. They did it without Brad or me expressing our gratitude nearly as much as we should have.

I thought about how different this visit might have been if my mother were still alive. She would have been living here for two years, fulfilling her self-proclaimed fantasy of a simpler life, hiking across the valley before coming home to read in front of the woodstove. Taking pictures, making friends with the locals, and meeting a good man for dinner at the Red Parka Pub. My brothers and I would converge for the holidays, ski on Christmas, and drink beer out of mason jars on New Year's. We'd be together and she'd be happy.

I shook the snow from my boots and walked into the house. The wind rattled the floor-to-ceiling windows in the living room. Mom would have filled the space with our worn-in leather couches, stained-glass lamps, photographs, candles, and sailing memorabilia. Other than the scratched kitchen table on which we'd eaten our cereal before school every morning, the downstairs was empty.

I pulled open the door to the basement and flipped on the light switch. Boxes labeled in her loose scrawl were stacked wall to wall, same as the last time I'd been here.

I billowed a trash bag and ripped the packing tape off the nearest box. It was not yet nine o'clock, but there was no time to waste. The town dump closed at three in the afternoon and we were determined to make this a one-day job, if only for the illusion of closure, for doing this and having done it.

The box sagged as I pulled at the tape, the cardboard wet beneath my fingers. The basement had flooded from a season of heavy rain and snow, and water had seeped into the bottom layer of boxes stacked near the door leading to the backyard. The sharp smell of mold hit my nostrils. I held my breath and pulled out my mom's blue floral sheets, heavy and damp. As I heaped them into a trash bag, what came to mind were not the childhood mornings I'd crawled in beside her warm body but the nights I'd slept alone in her bed while she was missing, sweating onto sheets now rank with mold.

I dumped a handful of dull silverware into a trash bag, setting aside a rusty butcher's knife to cut open the remaining boxes. I sliced open spines of clear packing tape to reveal my mother's towels, gardening gloves, seed packets, cookbooks, nautical charts, life jackets, Christmas lights, ceramic ornaments, old bank statements, fake flowers, faded paperbacks, records, sweaters, sail bags, salad bowls, wineglasses, sand dollars, lamps, sea glass, and CDs. Twenty trash bags were soon lined up at the foot of the stairs. The dump required garbage to be bagged rather than boxed, but I would have opened every single one of those boxes regardless. I needed to touch each memento before relinquishing it to a trash bag.

Her diploma: Boston College, class of '74. The macaroni angel I'd made her one year for Christmas. The construction paper booklet titled "1993 Mother of the Year," a Mother's Day present from my eight-year-old self. On the cover I'd drawn stick figures of my mom and me standing on the deck of *Pippins*. I opened the booklet and read what I'd written in pencil fourteen years earlier:

> My mom is special because I can depend on her anytime. She never tells lies to me. She cooks my food. Last night she gave me some strawberry rhubarb pie that she made. In the summer we like to go to the beach and Bensons Ice Cream. I love her a lot.

It was true, all of it. Until she threw me out of her apartment on New Year's, I could depend on her anytime. At twenty-two I loved her even more than an eight-year-old loves ice cream. *She never tells lies to me.* I set the book aside and stuffed everything else into a trash bag. Sentimentality wasn't going to bring her back. Renting a storage unit was only going to cost us.

We were eager to get the house off our hands. The chimney had collapsed earlier that winter and our Realtor had called at five in the morning to report that the North Conway fire department was up on the roof, shoveling ten-foot snowdrifts so that the whole thing wouldn't cave in.

While I was in the basement, Chris was up on the flat tin roof that extended over the porch, hacking away at three feet of ice and snow that had accumulated since the chimney's toppling. The poor design encouraged snow to accumulate rather than slide off.

I hauled two trash bags up the stairs and out to the U-Haul. I'd overfilled the bags and they kept smacking against my legs. Stepping off the porch, I glanced up at Chris on the roof. His jeans were soaked around the ankles and his hands bright red as he gripped the shovel. He rhythmically slammed its blunt metal blade, trying to break up the ice chunks that had latched on to the corrugated tin. He looked like he was freezing, but I knew he wouldn't come down until the job was done.

We worked through lunch, and by two o'clock the U-Haul was almost filled. Chris helped me carry the heavy stuff: two air conditioners, an old television, a stack of paintings, and Mom's brass bed frame. My brother labored up the stairs with an air conditioner. There was one more box tucked in an alcove under the stairs.

MVH PHOTOS was scrawled in blue permanent marker on the side: my mother's initials. This was the box that had sidetracked me on my first attempt at housecleaning a year and a half earlier. I knew opening it again would give Chris invitation to yell at me. The dump was closing in less than an hour. We were starting to complain as we passed on our way up and down the stairs, moaning that Brad should really be helping, secretly envious of him for having moved a safe distance away. Going through the photos would inevitably cause Chris to turn his frustrations on me, but I couldn't resist.

I reached in and pulled out a handful of glossy snapshots: *Pippins* flying a triangle of code flags between bow, mast, and stern. Mom swimming in Wickford harbor. My brothers and me lined up in the cockpit, grinning, me in a big straw hat, Brad in a PROUD TO BE AN AMERICAN T-shirt, and Chris shirtless and tanned. Ages six, seven, and ten. *Pippins*'s varnished cabin gleams behind our backs and we are invincible.

Chris came back down.

"We don't have time to look at those now," he said.

"Just a few."

Chris sighed and swung two trash bags over his shoulders, casting me a weary eye as he trudged up the stairs. I laid the photos back in the box and carried it out to Chris's car, sliding it into the backseat while he stood watching from the ramp of the U-Haul.

"What are you doing?"

"Keeping this."

"Where you going to put it?"

"Your house."

I walked back down to the basement before he had time to protest.

We finished loading the U-Haul in silence and rushed off to empty the truck. Fifteen minutes outside town, we passed through the gate leading into the dump. The snow was compacted with dirt, as if the very ground had been beaten. We circled a heap of bookshelves, desks, and dressers broken into planks and loose drawers. An enormous front-end loader barreled by us and made a left into a pit of trash.

Following a pickup truck up a hill that wound around the trash pit, we parked in a row of cars at the dumping area. It was like standing on Granite Pier and seeing the water swirling far below— a precipice above a valley of trash. The garbage would be tossed over the concrete ledge, falling ten stories to the raised snout of the loader down in the pit. The yellow beast would compact and haul the refuse away by the bucketful. Later it would be either buried or burned. Judging by the manmade hills surrounding the dump, my bet was on burial.

Walking the bags to the edge of the cutout and rolling them

over the edge would have meant continually climbing in and out of the truck bed. It was far more satisfying to stand in the back of the U-Haul and hurl the bags into the gaping mouth of the trash pit. Only the heavy ones needed to be carried to the edge. Chucking her stuff as hard as I could, my muscles ached, but there was a satisfying rhythm to it.

I swung back her bag of bedding and released it underhand. Then our Christmas ornaments. Strings of golden beads clanked against ceramic figurines as I pitched them out of the truck.

Chris followed my lead, giving me an approving nod as the bags were quickly disappearing. I kept waiting to feel some sense of relief from all this purging—wasn't that what my brothers were really hoping for when they claimed we'd run out of places to store our mother's belongings?

A middle-aged man in the pickup truck beside us upended his two barrels into the pit, a week of trash compared to our lifetime's worth. He walked over to the back of the U-Haul and peered in just as I was winding my arm back to toss *Pippins*'s old bowline.

"That's a perfectly good rope," he said.

I handed him the line. He put it in the bed of his pickup and saluted me as he drove off. I resumed my place in the back of the U-Haul, reaching for the nearest thing to get rid of.

Chris hauled the air conditioners to the edge and pushed them over one by one. I picked up my mom's favorite painting—an impressionistic gardener bent over a field of red peonies—and slowly walked to the edge of the truck. I didn't know who'd painted it, or where she'd gotten it, only that it had hung above the couch in our living room for most of my life. The country landscape suggested a cozy domesticity that I had no use for in the Providence apartment where I lived among strangers. I tossed the canvas into the trash pit and it looked for a moment as if the air was trying to lift it back up.

All that was left was the bed frame: two shiny brass arches. Chris took the headboard and I grabbed the foot. They were hollow and lighter than I thought a bed frame should be. We glanced around to make sure no one was watching, unsure of whether perfectly good furniture could really be left at the dump. The cars on either side of us had pulled away and we went for it. I clutched my mother's bed frame, knowing that this throw meant more than all the trash bags combined.

It was where she slept, where she dreamed, where she was most alone. Somewhere between imagining her new life in New Hampshire and making it a reality, even a good night's sleep had eluded her. Thrumming with anxiety, she'd gotten in her car instead. It was her bed, and I was about to throw it into a pit of trash.

I let it go and watched it cartwheel away from me, not knowing what it meant at all.

Down below, the loader geared up for another pass. It devoured our bags and went straight for the frame. Mom's headboard furiously tumbled toward the far side of the heap. The loader backed up, turned, and raised its extendable jaws. All that remained, when the beast wheeled away, was a mangled scrap of metal in a mountain of trash.

We returned the truck to the U-Haul rental center and got back in the Explorer.

I unlaced my boots and put my feet on the dashboard as Chris drove south. I was spent. When he reached to turn on the CD player, I demanded the radio, scanning through long stretches of static to briefly find sappy country songs until those too faded away.

Back on the one-lane highway, my cell phone started ringing. I knew it was Brad calling, and I knew he would keep calling until I answered.

"Hey, Brad."

"How'd it go?"

"Basement's empty."

"Sorry I wasn't there."

"I know."

"Hey, Linds?"

"What? We're about to stop for food."

"Thanks for doing this."

Reception was spotty along Route 16, and it was too hard to have a long conversation. I slid my phone into my pocket as Chris pulled into a Wendy's drive-thru.

I unwrapped his cheeseburgers while he got back on the road. He wolfed them down while I spooned up a Frosty.

"You okay?" he asked.

"I will be."

We drifted into silence. It was impossible to put into words what the day had meant to each of us. I kept telling myself that it was acceptable to throw out moldy sheets, even if they were my mother's. We had held on to the things that mattered.

I hoped Mom would be able to forgive us for the U-Haul, for the dump, for the house on the market, for not spreading her ashes yet, for graduating and getting married, for one-way tickets out of

Massachusetts, for doing and not doing what was needed in order to keep on living. I hoped she would understand.

A few hours later, we pulled into Chris's driveway.

"You can store that box in my basement," he said.

I wrapped my arms around the one box I'd thought worthy of saving. My arms were aching, but it felt good to be holding something solid. I bumped my way through the dark house to the basement stairs, clutching my wide-eyed self, my brothers, my mother, *Pippins, Chuckles, Mystery Girl,* the Atlantic, our everything. Hundreds of photos labeled in her hand: location, date, children's ages. I would stow the box in my brother's basement until I had a place of my own, a home for our past, with shelves for future albums. Maybe then I'd look at the pictures again—not to be reminded of all we'd lost but to remember what it felt like to be out on the ocean with my mother. What it meant to be floating with my best friend. If ever I was in doubt, I could turn to the pictures as evidence that pure happiness did exist; love like ours was true. And both would come again. All along we'd been doing what our mother had always taught us: surviving. But even more than that, it was time for my brothers and me to start living again.

I paused at the top of the stairs, my hands too full to flip on the light switch. I knew that if I set the box down, I wouldn't have the strength to pick it up again. Darkness would have to suffice. Holding tight, I felt for the first step.

Gratitude

THANK YOU TO my agent, Kris Dahl, and my editor, Colin Harrison, for believing in this project and making it better every step of the way.

To my mentors, then and now: Jeanne Caron, Donald Cameron, Laurie O'Neill, and Catherine Imbriglio, for showing me not where to go but how to get there.

I am indebted to many writers who helped me during my time at Columbia School of the Arts, and specifically to Lis Harris, Patty O'Toole, and Richard Locke.

Invaluable, each in their own way: Laura Magliochetti, Clara Orbe, Julia Alter, Kim Wayman, Laura Straub, Stephanie Barr, Elissa Bassist, Alex and Valerie Greenberg, Jill Rubin, Cassidy Metcalf, and Brian Brunault. There are others.

Impossible without my entire amazing family. To my brothers, Chris and Brad, thank you for your patience, your understanding, and your answers. And to my parents, for everything I don't know how to say, say love.

About the Author

Lindsay Harrison grew up in Massachusetts and attended Brown University and Columbia School of the Arts. She lives in Brooklyn, New York. This is her first book. Visit her website at LindsayHarrison.com.